PLAY THERAPY BASIC TRAINING WORKBOOK

A manual for learning and living
the Child-Centered Play Therapy philosophy

JODI ANN MULLEN PhD LMHC NCC RPT-S

So many great ideas put into action for skill development in child-centered play therapy, *and* perhaps even more important - for each therapist's personal self-development - to become more effective and efficient in providing CCPT! We especially like how this workbook:

- Intertwines the culture of childhood with Axline's Eight Principles to enhance and clarify the importance of the therapist's ability to show respect and provide deep empathy for the child's development and perspective.
- Provides concise and comprehensive information and easy-to-use exercises specifically written to supplement teaching and supervision of CCPT skills (structuring sessions, tracking, limit setting, responding to questions, reflecting feelings) and offers guidance for common challenges in CCPT sessions.
- Shares useful resources and reproducible handouts to use for weekly parent and teacher feedback, treatment planning, and video self-supervision.
- Offers insight and encouragement to those beginning to learn the value and healing power of CCPT.

-Nancy & Jeff Cochran, Department of Educational Psychology and Counseling at the University of Tennessee

Dr Jodi Mullen eloquently navigates the approach of Child Centred Play Therapy in such a way that readers new and familiar to the approach both benefit. Dr Mullen's commitment to providing valuable and clear information and examples in the workbook provide for an educational resource no play therapist can do without!

-Kylie Ellison (Founder & CEO of Centre for Play Therapy Australia)

Dr. Jodi Mullen's workbook on Child Centered Play Therapy is a valuable resource for both beginning and seasoned play therapists. Through easy to understand dialogue, examples, and space for practice, Dr. Mullen reminded me about the honor of working with kids: go easy on yourself if you are a parent and a play therapist, work diligently to avoid praise, create a space where kids are safe to make mistakes by acknowledging your own mistakes, and remember that it's the relationship between me and the child, and not the play, that truly makes a play therapy session. My favorite part of the workbook is the "nuts and bolts" resources: CCPT Implementation Checklists, Session Clinical Notes, Intakes, and my personal favorite (as a school counselor): Parent and Teacher reports. I wish I had this workbook in my own play therapy training years ago!

-Hennessey Lustica, PhD, LMHC (School Counselor & Counselor Educator)

It is not a substitute for appropriate professional preparation and/or clinical supervision.

ISBN: 978-0-9796287-3-3

The individual purchasing this book may reproduce items in the Appendix as needed for clinical use for his or her clients in accordance with "fair use" as defined in US/Copy Law.

ORDER INFORMATION:

Send any order requests to the attention of: Integrative Counseling Services, PLLC Continuing Ed Div.

5 W. Cayuga St. Oswego, NY 13126

TABLE OF CONTENTS

PLAY THERAPY BASIC TRAINING

Mental health and educational professionals who work with children can significantly benefit from training, supervision and clinical experience in play therapy. The most basic skills in play therapy can improve rapport and subsequently relationships with children (*professional AND personal*). This workbook will introduce or reinforce basic play therapy skills to engage children (from infancy through the elementary grades) in play therapy. Developmental and cultural issues relevant with this population will be addressed. Many practical and dynamic interventions are included. In reading and completing the exercises in this workbook, readers will be able to

1) Identify three distinct skills for using play therapy with children.

2) Identify the components of the Child-Centered play therapy philosophy.

3) Describe the Eight Basic Principles and give examples of attending skills that are consistent with the principles.

4) Use beginning play therapy skills to address the developmental and emotional needs of children.

INTRODUCTION

What is play therapy?

Play Therapy provides a context for understanding children and their worldviews. In this workbook the focus will be on Child-Centered Play Therapy. There are some elements of play therapy that are, however, consistent across theoretical and/or applied play therapy approaches. Although this workbook focuses on the Child-Centered philosophy and approach, much can be gleaned and applied to play therapy in general.

Play can be used in helping interventions with children to understand the perspectives, behaviors, feelings and thoughts of children (Ablon, 1996; Landreth, 2002; O'Connor, 2000; Orton, 1996). Many helping professionals use play within the context of the therapeutic session to establish rapport, to engage children, and to provide children with a way of expressing themselves that does not rely on receptive or expressive verbal skills beyond the child's developmental level (Ablon; O'Connor; Orton). Play therapy techniques differ from traditional verbal-based strategies of counseling and therapy. In play therapy, the helping professional relies on the child's play rather than on verbal responses as the communicative medium. "A child's play is his [*sic*] talk, and the toys are his [*sic*] words" (Ginott, 1961 p. 29). Children use play as one means of communicating their experiences (Axline, 1969; Landreth, 2002; Moustakas, 1953). The therapist who uses a play therapy intervention believes that children can communicate about their experiences through play. Engaging children in play therapy allows children to tell their stories and the therapist the opportunity to hear them. Keep in mind as you read and participate in this workbook, that the concept of working in a therapeutic relationship where children are allowed to play out their feelings, thoughts, and experiences is fundamental to the play therapist, no matter what theoretical orientation is adopted by the therapist.

What is a play therapist?

The Association for Play Therapy [APT] defines play therapy as, "The systematic use of a theoretical model to establish an interpersonal process wherein trained play therapists use the therapeutic powers of play to help clients prevent or resolve psychosocial difficulties and achieve optimal growth and development" (APT, n.d.). This definition specifies that the helping professional must be trained in play therapy. Those of us who do this work can tell you why that is…it's not easy to be a play therapist.

You may be using this workbook because, like so many of us who are doing play therapy, you recognized that the skills and attitudes necessary to work with children in counseling relationships are not typically found in most preparation programs in the helping professions (Landreth, 2002). I hope that you will use this workbook to reinforce what you have already learned in trainings, graduate coursework, clinical supervision and experience. This is not a substitute in any way for those educational and experiential elements of your training. If this is your introduction to play therapy, welcome! Now go out and get additional training, education, supervision and experience. I wholeheartedly endorse the words of Kottman (1999) when she asserts, "Counselors cannot learn how to effectively conduct play therapy simply by reading books or attending a workshop or two. This approach to counseling children requires an entirely different mind-set than talk therapy" (p.115). Effective counseling and play therapy with children requires more than an adaptation of skills, reading a book or attending a workshop.

Why can play therapy be considered cross-cultural counseling?

The relationship between client and counselor in play therapy shares many of the characteristics inherent in counseling relationships in general. Basic aspects of the counseling relationship, such as listening, empathy, and creating an atmosphere of trust and respect are present in the relationship between play therapist and client. However, there are several aspects of the counseling relationship that are relatively unique to counseling relationships with children, and especially the play therapy relationship (Mullen, 2003b).

The most important aspect of the counseling relationship from the client's perspective, the aspect that dictates whether the intervention is perceived and experienced as successful, is the counselor's ability to demonstrate understanding to the client. Counselors who work with children also have to demonstrate understanding in the context of the counseling relationship for it to be effective. Creating a counseling relationship in which the child client feels understood may be a more difficult task than in counseling relationships where the client is an adult. When the client in the counseling relationship is a child, aspects of the relationship are altered (Erdman & Lampe, 1996; Landreth, 2002; Thompson & Rudolph, 2000; Stern & Newland, 1994) and may make the task of empathizing with the client more daunting. Children differ from adults developmentally, cognitively, emotionally, physically and psychologically. These differences require counselors who work with children to have specialized knowledge. Erdman & Lampe (1996), suggest that it is also important to note that any cultural differences between counselor and client are likely to be enhanced by the differences accounted for by the assignment of status as adult or child.

Therapists and counselors who work with adults are not likely to encounter some of the weekly occurrences experienced by play therapists, such as a child who climbs the coat rack in the waiting area, or a client who spends the entire session talking about Sponge Bob®, or a client who is significantly below the therapist's level of cognitive and abstract reasoning ability (Landreth, 2002). Additionally, children are typically mandated clients in the sense that they did not request or seek out counseling services; another person (an adult) in their life initiated the relationship. Children, for the most part, do not even know why they are in the counseling relationship (Mullen, 2003b). We will explore the idea of childhood as a distinct culture throughout this workbook and how that impacts the therapeutic relationship between child and play therapist.

The Child-Centered approach

Like other theoretical approaches to play therapy, Child-Centered play therapists use play as a therapeutic medium for working with children (Axline, 1969; Kottman, 1999; Landreth, 2002; O'Connor, 2000; Thompson & Ruldoph, 2000). Child-Centered Play Therapy incorporates a developmental perspective for approaching and understanding children (Axline; Landreth; O'Connor). Axline is credited as the founder and developer of Child-Centered Play Therapy, and here's how she defined play therapy: (1947) "Play therapy is based upon the fact that play is the child's natural medium for self expression. It is an opportunity which is given to the child to 'play out' his feelings and problems just as, in certain types of adult therapy, an individual 'talks out' his difficulties" (p. 9). Axline argued that it was the relationship between child and therapist, and not the play, that made it therapy.

Child-Centered Play Therapy is an outgrowth of the person-centered theory (Rogers, 1951). Therefore, there exists a shared philosophical view with regard to the person-centered approach and Child-Centered Play Therapy. The Child-Centered approach is not made up of a series of techniques or procedures. It is grounded in the Child-Centered philosophy and thus is not merely a way of doing therapy, but a way of being. Therefore, if you do not believe in the philosophy, you cannot do Child-Centered Play Therapy.

In Child-Centered Play Therapy the relationship is key. The process and not the procedure characterize this approach (see page 13 in the workbook, or page 40 in the ebook, for an overview of the approach in comparison to other forms of play therapy). I will not offer you a comprehensive explanation of the approach here, but I will share the major theoretical constructs.

The Child-Centered approach believes that children will heal, grow and change if they are provided with an atmosphere where the pro-social aspects of self can flourish. This atmosphere is ideally created by the Child-Centered play therapist where trust and acceptance of the child is relayed, accurate empathic understanding is communicated, and allowance for the child to move at his or her own pace, in his or her own way is valued. Cornerstone to the Child-Centered philosophy is that the therapist is able to facilitate understanding by attempting to view the world from the child's frame of reference and phenomenological perspective (Killough McGuire & McGuire, 2001). It is a phenomenological and humanistic approach to helping that emphasizes the belief that people (including children) are striving toward actualizing self.

A WORD TO PARENTS AND CAREGIVERS WHO ARE STUDYING PLAY THERAPY....

I personally feel blessed that I learned about play therapy prior to becoming a parent. I was able to incorporate much of what I learned and believed about play therapy into my parenting style. I can tell you that although you would hear play therapy style limit setting and time structuring statements in my interactions with my children, you would also hear some yelling, impatience and lack of empathy. I practice being thoughtful, empathic, and accepting with my children, but sometimes I am not. The children in my playroom are my children for 30 minutes at a time, and usually no more than once a week. My children are my children forever and therefore our relationship is different. This will be the case with your children as well. You must be accepting of yourself before you can accept another.

I wanted to talk with you about this because many of my former students, who were already parents when they started play therapy training, have a strong reaction to the course content and experience. Many of them have expressed overwhelming feelings of guilt and even despair. They share that they made many mistakes in raising their children. All parents make mistakes with their children, even ones trained in play therapy. I guess I just wanted to make sure you keep in mind that no one does parenting (or anything else for that matter) perfectly. Again, remember you have to accept yourself before you can be accepting of someone else.

Sincerely,

RECIPE

~before starting this workbook~

Before you get started in this workbook, I would like you to take some time to think about the person you want to be in your relationships with children. Once you have cleared some space to focus on this, I would like you to use this page to articulate what you need to be that version of yourself. Please write those thoughts (and feelings?) down here in the form of a recipe.

Title:

Ingredients:

Directions:

Other notes (serving or storing suggestions, possible substitutions, where to find any elusive ingredients, etc…)

WHY EMPATHY

In this section of the workbook you will be working on communicating empathy. Play therapists need to be able to accurately communicate empathic understanding to children. It is one thing to make empathic responses, it's another to accurately communicate those responses. Child-Centered play therapists can demonstrate that they understand children, to children, through reflective responses. Reflections are a valuable skill to mental health professionals regardless of the age of their clients. You are likely to find reflecting the feelings of children to be inherently difficult because children do not typically have a wealth of words to express their feelings, and some children are reluctant or developmentally not prepared to put words to their experiences. In order to correctly reflect the feelings of children, it is important for play therapists to watch the child's facial expressions and body language. This will tell you more about what the child is feeling than what you will learn from watching what he or she is playing with. You can also learn a lot about how the child is feeling by listening to his or her breathing patterns and other bodily noises.

Sometimes you will make a reflection of feeling and you will be wrong (I do this at least once a session). These are terrific opportunities to demonstrate being a fallible human being. Additionally, children can clarify or correct you in these moments. That experience can be empowering for children as they recognize that they are indeed the experts of their internal experiences, including how they are feeling.

Reflection of Feeling

Reflection of feeling takes practice. It may feel unnatural and robotic at first. I recommend if you have pets that you practice reflective responses with them. Dogs are especially good partners in this learning endeavor: "Scamper, you look excited to see me." Now, I have cats and although this technique works with them, I tend to make the same reflective responses over and over: "Turnip, you are so sleepy right now." Have fun with this. Being able to accurately reflect feelings will benefit you in *all* of your relationships.

Reflection of feeling is a basic counseling skill. It is also a basic skill in play therapy. It is crucial that the Child-Centered play therapist be able to reflect the feelings of children. Reflecting feelings in children can be daunting because they are unlikely to verbally express their feelings.

It will take keen observation skills, such as paying close attention to the child's face to discern feelings in order to make a reflective response. It is through this skill that Child-Centered play therapists demonstrate to the child that they understand. Reflective listening also allows the play therapist to demonstrate accurate empathic understanding. An adequate number and variety of reflective responses are necessary to help children become aware of their emotions. It is this awareness of emotions that leads to the appropriate acceptance and expression of emotions (Ray, 2004).

Here are some examples of reflections of feeling:

> You are feeling frustrated.
>
> That was scary to you.
>
> You feel safe enough to try.

For the following responses please indicate with an "X" if the response is a reflection of feeling. If it is, replace the feeling word with another feeling word (I want you to grow your feelings vocabulary).

Example: You were worried. _X_ → You were concerned.

If it is not a reflective response (do not put an "X") try and change it into one.

Example: You built a tower. ___ → You feel proud of that tower

There are many possible correct answers. I will offer some in the answer key found in Appendix A.

1. You were very scared. ___ → _____

2. You want that toy. ___ → _____

3. That was surprising. ___ → _____

4. You are so tired. ___ → _____

5. You are sad. ___ → _____

6. That was a good one. ___ → _____

7. That shocked you. ___ → _____

8. You feel like a superhero. ___ → _____

9. You are angry. ___ → _____

10.   That was frustrating. ___ → _____

Reflecting Feeling: Let's practice

Here are several pictures of children. You have no context and no verbalizations. Try and reflect how the child is feeling based only on his or her facial expression… (Try to come up with three or more for each.)

Possible feelings:

_____

_____

_____

_____

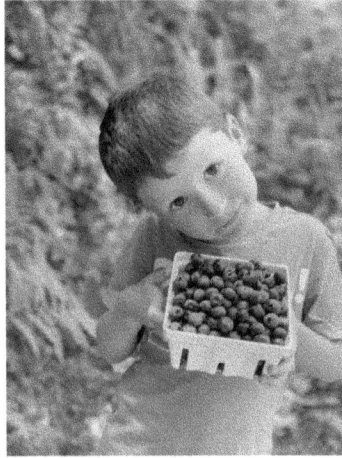

Possible feelings:

_____

_____

_____

_____

Possible feelings:

_____

_____

_____

_____

Possible feelings:

_____

_____

_____

_____

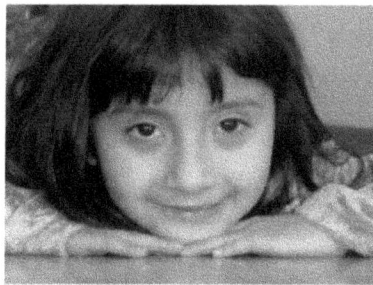

Possible feelings:

_____

_____

_____

_____

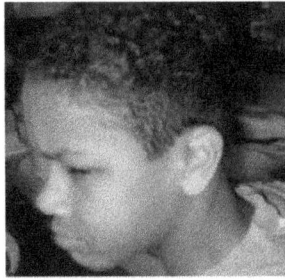

Possible feelings:

_____

_____

_____

_____

Feeling Words: Translations for Children

Directions: Create multiple ways of reflecting each feeling word listed to a young child.

Tip: Do not limit yourself to words. Facial expressions, large or small gestures, sound effects and interjections are all acceptable. Pair words and facial expressions, gestures, sound effects, or interjections for the most comprehensive communication. Sample answers can be found in Appendix A.

1. Annoyed _____

2. Ashamed _____

3. Bored _____

4. Brave _____

5. Cooperative _____

6. Curious _____

7. Defective _____

8. Disappointed _____

9. Disconnected _____

10. Enthusiastic _____

11. Frustrated _____

12. Hopeless _____

13. Insecure _____
14. Malicious _____
15. Obstinate _____
16. Overwhelmed _____
17. Satisfied _____
18. Tentative _____
19. Unpopular _____
20. Vulnerable _____

Empathizing versus Giving Solutions

Directions: Change the solution statement to an empathic statement. Example: It happens to everyone. → <u>You feel like you are the only one.</u> Sample answers can be found in Appendix A.

1. Don't cry. _____
2. Don't worry. _____
3. It will be okay. _____
4. It's not a big deal. _____
5. You can't win them all. _____
6. That's life. _____
7. It could be worse. _____
8. You'll do fine. _____
9. Everything will be all right. _____
10. It's not that important. _____
11. You'll get another chance. _____
12. Some problems solve themselves. _____
13. There's always a bright side. _____
14. People grow from experiences like this. _____
15. It's for your own good. _____

THE CHILD-CENTERED APPROACH

In this section, you will find exercises and discussion that are designed to ground you in the Child-Centered approach. We will spend some time addressing The Eight Basic Principles, comparing Child-Centered Play Therapy to other approaches, and how the Child-Centered Play Therapy approach is enhanced by viewing childhood as a culture.

The Eight Basic Principles

The basic principles that guide the Child-Centered play therapist are very simple, but they are incredible in their possibilities when followed sincerely, consistently, and intelligently by the play therapist.

The principles are as follows:

1. The play therapist must create a warm and friendly relationship with the child. Good rapport is established as soon as possible.
2. The play therapist accepts the child exactly as she is.
3. The play therapist establishes a feeling of permissiveness in the relationship so that the child feels free to express his feelings.
4. The play therapist recognizes the feelings the child is expressing and reflects those feelings back to her in such a way that she gains insight into her behavior.
5. The play therapist has a strong respect for the child's ability to solve his own problems if given an opportunity to do so. The responsibility to make choices and to change is the child's.
6. The play therapist does not attempt to direct the child's behaviors or verbalizations in any way. The child leads the way and the play therapist follows.
7. The play therapist does not attempt to hurry the child along. Play therapy is a gradual process and is honored as such by the play therapist.

8. The play therapist establishes only those limitations that are necessary to ground the child to the world of reality and to make the child aware of her responsibility in the relationship.

Adapted from: Axline, V. (1969), *Play therapy.* Cambridge, MA: Houghton Mifflin

Child-Centered Play Therapy: The Relationship

The relationship between the child and the play therapist is cornerstone to the child's growth. The Child- Centered Play Therapy philosophy is as important (if not more) than any one particular skill.

The following table summarizes the basic tenets of Child-Centered Play Therapy in relation to other therapeutic approaches.

Child-Centered		Other approaches	
Here and Now	vs	**There and Then**	In Child-Centered Play Therapy what is happening in the moment is what is important. What has happened in the past and what will happen in the future is not the focus of the intervention. The temporal focus is in the present.
Developmental	vs	**Remedial**	Child-Centered play therapists believe in a growth model. People, including children, grow so trying to remediate and change them is not part of the approach; facilitating growth and development is.
Person	vs	**Problem**	The child is the center of the Child-Centered Play Therapy intervention and not the diagnosis, behavior, academic or social problem.
Affect	vs	**Cognition & Behavior**	Child-Centered play therapists focus on how children feel and aspire to accurately communicate empathic understanding.
Understanding	vs	**Explaining**	For Child-Centered play therapists understanding the phenomenological perspective of the child is far more important than being able to explain the child's behaviors.
Accepting	vs	**Correcting**	In Child-Centered Play Therapy the therapist accepts the child exactly as he is. It is not the job of the play therapist to take a corrective stance in the relationship with the child.
Therapist as a person	vs	**Therapist as an expert**	The Child-Centered play therapist is a fallible human being and genuine adult in the child's life. The play therapist is not the expert on the child; the child is.
Spontaneity	vs	**Structure**	The child is the director of the session, so Child-Centered Play Therapy sessions are structured by the child. The playroom toys used and/or the activities engaged in are chosen by the child.
Action	vs	**Talk**	The child communicates through play so talk, although a viable means of communication, is not necessary.
Attitude change	vs	**Behavior change**	Child-Centered play therapists believe that attitude change is the most salient and significant form of change. Observable changes will come after attitude change.
Child's direction	vs	**Therapist's instruction**	The child directs and takes responsibility for the content of the session. The Child-Centered play therapist keeps the space safe and does not direct the child's play in any subtle or obvious manner.
Child's wisdom	vs	**Therapist's knowledge**	Child-Centered play therapists regard each child as the expert of her own experience. The culture of childhood is respected and valued. Child-Centered play therapists have a great deal to learn from their clients.

Adapted From:

Landreth, G. (2002). *Play therapy: The Art of the relationship(2nd ed.)*. New York: Brunner-Routedge.

Living the Philosophy

As stated previously, the Eight Basic Principles as created by Axline (1947), are the basis for Child- Centered Play Therapy. These principles seem simple but require a philosophical grounding in Child- Centered beliefs. The purpose of this exercise is to have you focus on the philosophy.

Please review the Eight Basic Principles on page 12, or pages 37-38 in the ebook, and answer the following questions accordingly.

Review each principle.

1. How do you implement these principles in your current interactions with children?

    A. Are there any that you don't implement?

    i. What gets in your way?

    ii. How could you implement the principle?

2. Review each principle. Do you implement any of the Eight Basic Principles in your everyday life?

    A. If yes, which ones, and how? B. If no, what gets in your way?

    i.How would it impact your relationships if you did follow the principles?

    ii.State here how you will begin to incorporate one of the eight principles in your everyday life.

3. Review each principle. Which of the Eight Basic Principles would be least difficult for you to follow? Why?

4. Review each principle. Which of the Eight Basic Principles would be most troublesome for you to follow? Why?

5. Review each principle. Which of the Eight Basic Principles do you need the people in your life to follow to feel more supported?

    A. How can you communicate this?

6. Review the principles. Think about your childhood. Is there someone who seemed to follow these principles in their interactions with you?

    A. If yes, what was that like?

    B. If no, what do you imagine would have been different if someone had?

7. Communicate the Eight Basic Principles philosophy to someone who supports your work. What is/was it like to talk about it?

Childhood as a Culture

I have described in various parts of this workbook that it is essential to view childhood as a distinct culture in order to truly be effective as a play therapist. Here are several elements that comprise culture and sub-culture and how they are constructed. This is a complex perspective. It may take multiple attempts at these exercises before you are able to make a strong argument for childhood as a distinct culture. What examples can you think of that provide evidence for the stance that childhood is a culture?

RULES are the cultural components that guide conduct and actions. What are two of the rules specific to the culture of childhood?

_____

_____

_____

_____

Possession is the law. If you have it in your hand it is yours.

Finders keepers, losers weepers. This is similar to the first example in that if an item is in your possession, it belongs to you.

Utensils for eating your food are optional.

I do not know if these rules differ all that much from the rules of adulthood; however, in adulthood these rules are covert.

VALUES are ideas that do not require external proof to be considered true. Values define the boundaries of cultures by aiding in communication because they are shared among group members. Values are often sources of disagreement between cultural groups, as each group experiences the situation from their own perspective (Pederson & Ivey, 1993).

Identify two values that are shared among people whose most salient cultural affiliation is childhood.

_____

_____

_____

Pederson & Ivey (1993) offer this example in demonstrating the value differentials and how they can be a source of conflict between the cultures of adulthood and childhood. Children may experience homework from a short-term perspective and as taking away from free time. Parents (members of the culture of adulthood) may view homework differently through a long-term lens where the benefits are longstanding.

In the culture of childhood the perception of time has a great deal to do with values. Because the temporal focus of children is in the present, their values will represent this perspective. Think of the potential disagreements between the cultural groups of adulthood and childhood with regard to these statements:

"Hurry up - we only have three minutes." "You are taking too long."

"Please one more minute." "You said, in a few minutes."

CUSTOMS are also elements of culture. They are best described as longstanding practices or conventions that regulate social life.

Can you name three customs practiced in the culture of childhood?

_____

_____

_____

_____

Many childhood games could be considered in this section. Selection of teams through "One potato, two potato..." or "Rock, paper, scissors," serve as examples.

LANGUAGE comprises the various communicative mediums present in the culture. What are some communications that are specific to the culture of childhood?

_____

_____

_____

_____

It is a perfectly acceptable practice to make up words in the culture of childhood, although this is not the case in adulthood. At four, my daughter was trying to communicate to her father and me that she was annoyed and felt the situation she was in was unfair. She turned to us and said, "I just think this whole thing is *impurtutious.*" In that moment we were able to speak her cultural language and demonstrated that we understood her plight through reflection of feeling although neither of us had heard this word uttered before. We did not correct her as adults typically do.

Another example that stands out among children is the ability of older children to understand the language of younger children of which adults are not privy.

STATUS - The cultural component of status speaks to the value of members in the culture particularly in contrast to the dominant culture.

How is status determined within the culture of childhood? Write down two examples.

_____

_____

_____

_____

Size matters, and children who are taller and/or look older (more like members of the dominant culture) seem to achieve higher status within the culture of childhood. Status also comes with knowledge of the dominant culture. Children who know about, or have experiences with, elements of adolescent or adulthood cultures achieve higher status in their own culture.

VIEW OF DOMINANT CULTURE: ADULTHOOD - If childhood is a culture, then the dominant culture would be the culture of adulthood. It is reasonable to believe that there exists a shared view of dominant culture.

Name three separate perspectives possibly held by members of the culture of childhood about members of the culture of adulthood.

_____

_____

_____

_____

Adults have different rules for children than they do for members of their own culture.

Adults can lie and there are no consequences, as in the examples of the tooth fairy, Santa Claus, and the boogie man.

Adults believe they know better about the internal states of children, which lead to such utterances as, "How can you be hungry? You just ate" or, "Put your jacket on. I am cold."

Another reason it is an awesome responsibility (and honor) to be a play therapist:

Skilled play therapists will be able to effectively navigate the cultural barriers between adulthood and childhood. Because of this unique skill, play therapists should anticipate a more complex role in their relationships with children. Play therapists will have the added responsibility to serve as translators between the two cultures (Mullen, 2003b).

Child Centered Play Therapy Advantages and Disadvantages

It is likely that you will be challenged by people when you use an approach that has the word "play" in it. Play therapists frequently find themselves defending the play therapy approach in clinical settings with both professionals and other people involved in the lives of their children clients. It is important for play therapists to be familiar with the research literature that supports play therapy as an evidenced-based and science-based approach to therapy.

When helping professionals primarily use the child centered play therapy approach these questions about the permissiveness and child-direction are additional aspects that child centered play therapists can anticipate. The same advice holds true here; you must familiarize yourself with the research literature so you can articulate your clinical decision to use child centered play therapy. The following section is a quick snapshot of what some of the advantages and limitations are of the child centered play therapy approach (some apply to play therapy in general too).

Advantages

Children feel empowered to make decisions and choices.

Because change is made by the child, at the child's pace, it is likely to be sustained.

Children learn how to solve their own problems.

Children feel unconditionally accepted.

Play therapy is often a comfortable setting for children; it is non-stigmatizing.

Children get to play. They choose what to play and how to play. Self-directed learning happens in this context.

And as a bonus... In child centered play therapy, the play therapist gets to be playful.

Limitations

Children's play is symbolic and therefore you may not know if what is being played out is an accurate portrayal of what children are experiencing.

It can be challenging to convert the language of play. This can pose a limitation in court testimony or even in consultation with parents and other professionals.

Child centered play therapy, like other forms of play therapy and therapy in general, is a process. It takes time and is not a quick fix.

The way positive results and change are measured in therapy may be difficult to detect and document when using the child centered play therapy approach.

What will happen when you mix it together: The Culture of Childhood and the Eight Basic Principles

Listed below are the Eight Basic Principles (yes again, because I want you to become well-acquainted with them). For each principle I will discuss how viewing childhood as a distinct culture will factor into the practical application of the principle. I have given an example of what this principle might look like in a session. As you are thinking about these principles and examples, try and formulate your own examples from your clinical, personal or professional experiences.

1. The play therapist must create a warm and friendly relationship with the child. Good rapport is established as soon as possible.

> *When I work with children I am aware of the cross-cultural relationship. I am a representative from the culture of adulthood. In order to develop a relationship quickly with a child I must be able to transverse cultural barriers and present myself in a way that demonstrates that I honor their culture. The fastest, most salient way to do this is to meet the child at their physical level. Therefore, when I greet my client I am sure*

to crouch down so I can be at her level. Additionally, children are incredible readers of non-verbals. When I meet with a child I am sure to smile warmly as I greet them.

Parent: "Say hi to Dr. Jodi. She is going to help you."

PT (crouching down to the child's level, smiling, and speaking to the child): "Hi Sammy, let's spend some time playing today. You can call me Jodi. Mom, we will see you in a little while after Sammy and I have played."

Your example: _____

_____

_____

2.　The play therapist accepts the child exactly as she is.

Our adulthood cultural counterparts often communicate to children that they are not okay. In Child-Centered Play Therapy it is important to communicate that children are okay just the way they are. None of us wants to be defined by our behaviors - that is something our two cultures have in common. Our culture tends to view children and childhood through that lens. As part of a marginalized culture, children's perspectives, thoughts, feelings and behaviors are often minimized or denied by the dominant (adult) culture, therefore communicating that people from their culture (childhood) are not accepted. For example, if a child says, "I hate my sister," rather than demonstrate that we accept how she is feeling about her sister in the moment we correct, "You don't hate your sister." Consequently, the adult has just implied, "I know more about how you are feeling than you do AND I do not accept how you are feeling."

Child: "I hate you. I do not want to stay in your stupid playroom."

PT: "You are really mad at me right now and want me to know what it's like to have hurt feelings."

Your example: _____

_____

_____

3.   The play therapist establishes a feeling of permissiveness in the relationship so that the child feels free to express his feelings.

> *From the perspective of the culture of childhood, our culture of adulthood must seem so restrictive. There are rules and structure in many interactions between our two cultures. Seldom does the representative from the culture of childhood have any say in the negotiation of these implicit and explicit relational rules. Therefore, their perspectives and experiences are not given the space to emerge and be shared when our two cultures engage in relationships.*

PT: "Jessie this is a very special room. You can do almost anything in this room. If there is something you cannot do, I will tell you. You can also say anything."

Child: "If I say a bad word you will not like me."

PT: "It's hard for you to trust what I am saying. Jessie, you can say anything in this room."

Your example: _____

_____

_____

4.   The play therapist recognizes the feelings the child is expressing and reflects those feelings back to her in such a way that she gains insight into her behavior.

> *Too often children's feelings are minimized or denied by even caring and thoughtful people whose primary cultural*

identification is that of adulthood. When we deny and minimize the feelings of children, they likely feel that we do not understand or even worse, do not care. Here's a classic example: A child falls and gets hurt, scrapes his knee. The child is crying and the adult responds, "You're ok, that wasn't so bad." What if the adult recognized and honored the child's feelings? Maybe then the reply would go something like this, "You fell down and that hurt."

Child: "It's not fair that I cannot stay longer."
PT: "You feel mad and disappointed that our time is up."

Your example: _____

_____

_____

5. The play therapist has a strong respect for the child's ability to solve his own problems if given an opportunity to do so. The responsibility to make choices and to change is the child's.

In our culture of adulthood we can never seem to move fast enough. When we are interacting with people from the culture of childhood we often forget that in their culture things are not so rushed. There's a physical component to this too. Just watch adult-child dynamics when out walking. Children can only walk so fast, as the strides of preschoolers are likely to be a third of the stride of an adult. We rush children in so many circumstances particularly in situations where there are problem-solving opportunities. Consequently, if we always solve children's problems for them, they will have little experience with, or tolerance for frustration. As children grow they become accustomed to having their problems solved for them. Additionally, they will be unfamiliar with the feeling of pride when they recognize they are capable.

Child: "I cannot open this." PT: "It is so frustrating." Child: "I hate this thing."
PT: "You got really mad and decided not to keep trying."

Your example: _____

_____

_____

6.   The play therapist does not attempt to direct the child's behaviors or verbalizations in any manner. The child leads the way and the play therapist follows.

> *In Child-Centered Play Therapy the child gets to make the decisions and lead the way. Children do not have much experience with this relationship dynamic in the context of a relationship with an adult. Some children will be suspicious, others will test it out, and still others will be scared and/or perplexed and look for your direction. In fact, children are often confused when they are in a relationship with an adult and the adult does not set the agenda or direct their play. A quick story: A seven year old girl that I had been seeing in play therapy for almost six months had initially started off tentatively in the playroom. I reflected often to her in those early sessions that she was feeling unsure about me, the room, herself. After much testing and just as much consistency she realized I was truly going to let her run the show. She created a role play scenario and directed me to be the witch, and she was the princess. Shortly after the role play began, she in her princess crown and me in my witch's hat, she turned to me and said, "Ok now I need you to pretend you are a grown up." Recognizing that I had truly crossed the line into the culture of childhood I responded, "I bet I can do that."*

Child: "I don't know what to do. What should I do?" PT: "You feel pressured to decide."

Child: "Yeah, just tell me, pick something."

PT: "It's strange when adults don't tell you what to do." Child: "Can't you just be the boss and tell me."

PT: "Selina, in this room you can choose to do almost anything."

Your example: _____

_____

_____

7. The play therapist does not attempt to hurry the child along. Play therapy is a gradual process and is honored as such by the play therapist.

As was stated earlier in this discussion, the culture of childhood does not share the same conceptualization of time as the culture of adulthood. Furthermore, the Child-Centered philosophy is consistent with the notion that therapy, just like growth, healing, and change, happens gradually. Play therapy is a gradual process. Many adult folk would like you to fix the children you are working with and there seems to be an arbitrary time in which that "fixing" is supposed to happen. The notion of fixing is inconsistent with the Child-Centered philosophy as is the notion of time constraints. There are, of course, time constraints, but you cannot rush the process of therapy. Because you are a genuinely helpful and caring person you may feel like you can do some other "things" to speed progress in children along. However, when you do that you are not respecting the notion of time (and certainly development) in the culture of your client, childhood. Just a quick illustration: My favorite meal is roast turkey. The thing with roast turkey is that I only eat it a few times a year because in my family it's served on holidays (my mouth is watering just thinking about it). Now, I am fairly certain that you can *microwave a turkey and it will indeed be cooked and cooked quickly; however, I am only interested in what results from the **process** of cooking the turkey slowly for hours. See my point?*

Child enters the playroom and stands in the middle of the room. PT: "You look like you don't feel like playing."

Child nods affirmatively.

PT: "You are going to take your time in here." Child nods affirmatively.

Your example: _____

_____

_____

8.   The play therapist establishes only those limitations that are necessary to ground the child to the world of reality and to make the child aware of her responsibility in the relationship.

Children must think we adults are hypocritical people. Our culture possesses very different rules for the members of our culture then it does for members of the culture of childhood. For instance, in our culture it is okay to lie and say, "No, you don't look fat." Yet if children lie while interacting with our culture, it is a punishable offense. Adults are inconsistent in their interactions with children. Children need us to be consistent and to help them contain when they are feeling out of control. Limit setting allows us to provide that level of support without setting what must seem to them like arbitrary and hypocritical rules. In the therapeutic playroom limits are set to help children stay safe, to help you remain safe and to maintain the safety of the physical setting. Limits are set in Child- Centered Play Therapy in such a way that children can make decisions about their behavior because they know what the consequence will be and that other choices exist.

When the play therapist uses limit setting skills in the playroom, the child learns that this adult means what they say. If you set only the necessary limits, children are likely to respect your rules because by setting only those necessary limits you have demonstrated your respect for them. Children subsequently learn that you will indeed be there for them even when they make poor choices with regard to safety and that your relationship is strong enough to withstand mistakes. Limit setting is the most difficult skill in Child- Centered Play Therapy. Expect that this will take a great deal of practice.

Child: pulls the play therapist's hair

PT: "Brianna, remember I told you there are some things you cannot do in here. You cannot pull my hair. You wanted me to feel hurt. You can pull the doll's hair."

Child: pulls the play therapist's hair again

PT "Brianna you are so mad and you want to hurt me. You cannot pull my hair, and if you do it again our time will be up for today. You can choose to pretend to pull my hair and I'll act like it hurts bad."

Your example: _____

_____

_____

GUIDELINES

This is the section where you will find examples, exercises, and commentary designed to structure your experience in the playroom. I will give overt and explicit instructions and lay out a clear format for play therapy sessions. When you start out on this journey you might want to stick to the instructions in this section verbatim. Adhering to the model provided will make many of the complexities that emerge in the playroom easier to handle. Later, when you have more training, supervision and experience, you can put your own unique spin on what you say and do within the framework of Child-Centered Play Therapy. In the beginning, if you stick to the explicit instructions and scripts you will find it easier to manage the nuances that develop as you integrate the philosophy and the approach.

Toy List

On the following pages you will find a recommended list of toys for the therapeutic playroom. There are several reasons why toys are chosen for the playroom. They should be sturdy and durable so that children can use them without being overly concerned about damaging them. Toys should also be inexpensive and easy to replace. It is important that the play therapy room is a consistent place (within the limits of reality). The same toys should be in the room each time, so you want toys that are durable and easy to replace if they break or get damaged. Expensive toys or toys that hold special meaning for you do not belong in the playroom. The presence of these toys in the playroom will likely be distracting to you and may prevent you from sticking to the Eight Basic Principles. Furthermore, the toys in the playroom should allow for expression of feelings including regression and aggression. Children in play therapy will express, regress, and aggress, and you want to supply toys such that they can communicate these experiences.

The toy list that follows will get you started. I have included a commentary to explain why the listed toy is viewed as important with regard to the play therapy playroom. I have also included some additional discussion regarding certain toys that are particularly useful. I have learned about these toys from the most reliable sources - children.

- **Blocks:** Children can build and create whatever they choose in the playroom. I recommend foam blocks because they stand up well and are less likely to injure you or the child if they come falling down or get thrown at you. They are expensive, but hold up well and are even waterproof.

- **Mirror:** Children like seeing what they look like. It is particularly fascinating to them as they try out the various aspects of their personality. Non-breakable mirrors are available at a variety of retail stores.

- **Ball:** A ball that is not hard is your best bet here (see rationale regarding foam blocks). Children will often use a ball to bring you into the relationship through catch or other play that requires the play therapist to participate. It is a great tool for children to communicate about relationships and competency.

- **Family/ People Puppets:** I need to tell you that I am not a puppet person and I am afraid that I send this vibe out to my clients. The children I work with rarely use puppets. I know from talking with many colleagues that this is not their experience. I just thought I should be upfront with you so that you can filter my discussion about puppets through that knowledge. There are two puppets in my playroom that are used regularly (even with my negative puppet vibe). Both puppets are menacing; a dragon puppet and a crocodile puppet. It is important to have a varied collection (which I do). It is also important to have puppets whose mouths are not sewn shut. Children give voices to puppets (or vice versa) so when the mouth is sewn shut it is difficult for communication to take place.

- **Dollhouse:** You might check with friends or colleagues who have children to see if they have used dollhouses that they would be willing to pass on. Consignment stores or garage sales are also good places to look for dollhouses. I recommend this because a dollhouse can be one of the more expensive items in the playroom. Here again, you are looking for something sturdy. Dollhouses are a great inclusion in the playroom. Essentially, the dollhouse allows the child to communicate about what happens or happened, or what they wish would happen or had happened at home. It's a way to visit a child's home from their phenomenological perspective.

- **Foam Noodles:** Foam noodles are inexpensive water toys. They are approximately five feet long and made of lightweight foam material. They come in a variety of colors. A very creative play therapist, Pam Gicale, cuts these noodles in half, so now there are two 2.5 feet foam cylinders in lieu of swords or other weapons. This idea is brilliant, and here's why: 1) It hurts a lot less when you get hit, poked or otherwise struck with a noodle, 2) they are very inexpensive, 3) they last and last, so they are a great investment and finally, 4) they are acceptable in playrooms where overt toy weapons would not otherwise be allowed.

- **Egg cartons (empty, of course):** Any empty box like a cereal box will do. The purpose of including this item in the playroom is connected to limit setting. Often children will want to break or destroy something. They may feel enraged or just want to communicate to you what it is like to have something you value damaged beyond repair. Clearly, children cannot be permitted to break toys in the playroom. They can, however, be redirected through limit setting to items such as empty egg cartons or cereal boxes that they can destroy without the emotional consequences of feeling guilty, scared or threatened. It allows you to remain centered in the Eight Basic Principles as you can accept the child's feelings, but keep the session grounded in reality.

- **Tea Party Set:** A tea set is another toy that allows for relational themes to emerge. It is also a useful way for children to communicate about nurturance and connection.

- **Washable Magic Markers® and Paint:** Art supplies allow for expression. I recommend washable markers or paint because they allow me to worry less about the ramifications of children getting their clothes or bodies marked up. It is important to note that washable does not apply to every fabric or surface. In my experience even washable markers or paint leave a trace on skin.

- **Baby Bottle:** The perfect toy for children to express needs or desires to regress. Keep your baby bottle filled with water. Children appreciate being able to "be a baby" without the typical negative reaction they may get from adults and other children outside of the playroom. As with any toy that children put in their mouths, take care to sanitize.

- **Farm Animals:** Children can use farm animals in traditional ways. It may be less threatening to demonstrate relational patterns using animals rather than people (Kottman, 2003). Therefore, having animal figures allows children the opportunity to communicate about people without having to do so directly.

- **Telephone (2):** Telephones are wonderful metaphors for communication. In the playroom I like to have two, so if the child wants to include me in the play, it is easily done. When children use the phone in the playroom, I want to be alert to who they are calling, who they are talking to, who they cannot get connected with and certainly how they are responding verbally and non-verbally.

- **Play Doh®/ Clay:** Play Doh® or modeling clay are nice additions to a playroom. Children can use these mediums to create almost anything. The tactile experience alone can be very powerful for some children. If you have carpeted floors, be thoughtful about how you limit the use of these materials. It is also reasonable to limit mixing Play Doh® and clay with water, sand or paints so that it will last longer and will not need to be replaced as often. Also, there are some of you who cannot handle even the thought of having your Play Doh® colors mixed together. If this is the case, you may want to have two separate containers, one for Play Doh® that cannot be mixed with other colors and one for Play Doh® that can be mixed. Again, your idiosyncratic behaviors will get in the way of adhering to the Eight Basic Principles. Therefore, it behooves you to be thoughtful about the process so that you can be comfortable, permissive and therapeutic.

- **Army Men:** By the way, where are the army women? Small figures are useful to children because they are easy to manipulate. Toy soldiers can help children communicate about group dynamics, fear, protection and safety.

- **Doctor's Kit:** A good medical kit for the playroom can be difficult to find. I don't want one that contains toy medical instruments that are battery operated or make specific noises. I like to leave the creativity up to the child. It is reasonable to create your own medical kit. You can purchase working stethoscopes for about $10.00, and bandages, cotton balls, and medicine droppers can also be purchased for little expense. A working stethoscope is priceless in the playroom, as children can figuratively "check you out," even on the inside. They can also check on themselves this way. The stethoscope allows for the communication of trust, nurturance, relationship, and boundary themes. Bandages in the playroom are like gold to children. For some reason we in the adult culture tend to hoard bandages and drive up their perceived value. Children love using bandages in the playroom and often communicate hurt, trust, self-care and empathy through their play with this item. I do limit the number I have in the playroom at any one time. It seems no matter what the amount in the playroom, whether one or ten, they all get used.

- **Baby Doll:** It's important to have a baby doll (even better to have two) in your therapeutic playroom. Children are able to communicate vast amounts of information about their perspectives including, but not limited to, themselves, their families, how they view younger children, nurturance and care taking/giving through play with dolls. Play therapists can honor diversity by having baby dolls that are representative of the multicultural, diverse society we live in.

- **Camera:** A toy camera is sometimes difficult to find because many of them have images already programmed so what the child sees when he looks through the lens has already been decided. I prefer real cameras without batteries or film. These are easy to find and inexpensive, and the 35 mm models are available for less than $2.00. Cameras allow children to demonstrate what they want to remember. Cameras are fine vehicles for the communication of important themes in play therapy like memory, regression, relationships, and resilience.

- **Paper:** I want to have paper in the playroom as a means for children to create what they want or need. I do limit the paper to three pieces because I have had experiences where there has been a large stack of paper and a child has scribbled on every page. That might not be a big deal to you, but what happened for me was that I got irritated and then was not able to adhere to the Eight Basic Principles.

- **Dinosaurs:** Dinosaurs can be menacing and are therefore useful for the child to communicate fear or anger. They can also be used by children in the playroom to communicate about relationships (refer to the discussion regarding farm animals).

- **Bop Bag:** Some professionals do not believe that a bop bag is an appropriate toy to have in the playroom. The rationale of this argument is that the bop bag serves to increase aggression. My experience has been the contrary. It's true that many children use the bop bag to demonstrate aggression but it is also regularly used to protect, defend, or befriend children in the playroom. Finding a bop bag that is durable enough to withstand several aggressive children per week is a challenge. There are definitely some that hold up better with regular and frequent use, and I would recommend seeking them out.

In-Home Based Play Therapy Toy List

Many mental health practitioners provide in-home based services. This list was created for professionals who use a play therapy approach in the context of in-home services. This list is not exhaustive, although should provide a foundation.

Some overall considerations for In-Home Based Play Therapy sessions:

- toys/materials should be light in weight and simple to transport
- toys/materials should be inexpensive but durable
- toys/materials should be easy to clean up and pack up
- choice of toys/materials should be considered through a cultural lens that factors in that you will be in the child's home

The list of toys/materials:

- a tote for carrying your supplies can also double as a play kitchen (For an examples checkout Pintrest DIY boards)
- empty egg cartons, cereal boxes, spice containers (Even cleaned out these will retain scent. This is one way to weave cultural thoughtfulness into sessions.)
- paper, plastic or other light weight cups, plates, utensils
- baby doll
- baby bottle
- soft ball (like Nerf-brand)
- plain paper
- washable magic markers
- bandages (as many as you have will get used, so I usually have 3-5 available per session)
- empty vitamin bottle (washed out thoroughly, of course)
- stethoscope (you can get real working ones for about $10, worth it!)
- doll house or other people figures
- toy cars (2-4, various sizes and styles)
- emergency vehicle
- menacing character puppet
- nurturing character puppet
- play handcuffs
- jump rope
- mask (a variety is good, like 2-3)

You can always add your favorites and cater specifically to the population of children you work with. This list is most appropriate for play therapists using a Child-Centered approach. Finally, remember that you want toys that will allow children to express, regress, and aggress in their play.

Tracking

Tracking is another useful skill in the play therapy session. It is a simple response that verbally documents what the play therapist is observing. Simply stated, a tracking response *tracks* the behaviors of the child in the play therapy session. By tracking the child's behavior, the play therapist proves to the child that the play therapist is attentive and accepting. According to Ray (2004) tracking responses also serve to immerse the play therapist in the child's world and experience. This skill is critical to the play therapy process and is the most basic of skills utilized in the playroom. Tracking responses need to be balanced with higher-level play therapy skills such as reflection of feeling (see the section on empathy that begins on page 24).

Here are some behaviors that are frequently displayed in a play therapy session. In the space provided, make a tracking response. Sample tracking responses can be found in Appendix A.

Example: Child picks up baby bottle and looks at it. <u>You wanted to check that out.</u>

1. Child stands on the chair. _____

2. Child jumps up and down. _____

3. Child uses toy food to "feed" the baby doll._

   _____

4. Child tries several crayons.

   _____

5. Child looks out the window after hearing a sudden noise.

   _____

How to Set Limits in a Play Therapy Session

Limits in play therapy are rules or guidelines for behavior. They are explicitly defined and enforced by imposing consequences or results if the rule is broken.

The rationale for setting limits in Child-Centered Play Therapy is grounded in the belief that children need help to define their boundaries, feel safe, and to simultaneously be able to explore their environment and try out behaviors.

Setting limits in Child-Centered Play Therapy allows children to learn that what happens to them is a direct consequence of their behavior. They can begin to take responsibility for their actions through the proper limit-setting and consequences.

Consider these factors before making a limit:

1. Is this limit necessary for the safety of the child?
2. Is this limit necessary for the safety of others?
3. Is this limit necessary for the protection of property?
4. Is this limit enforceable?

Why set as few limits as possible?

1. Children cannot be expected to remember many rules.
2. If only necessary boundaries are imposed, the child can explore the situation and can truly lead the way.
3. Since consistency is important (and you want to be viewed as a person who means what he says), the fewer the limits imposed, the more likely it is that the limits will be enforced every time they are broken.

Steps in setting limits:

1. Determine if a limit is necessary. Here are some examples of limits in the playroom:

   a. Nothing should be thrown at the mirrors, video camera, or windows.
   b. No hurting the play therapist or self (child).
   c. No sharp objects should be directed at the bop bag.
   d. The room should not be left during the session except for one trip to the bathroom.

It's critical that children stay in the playroom so that they can engage in the therapeutic process, remain physically safe, and confidentiality can be maintained. It is likely that children will need to leave to use the bathroom. Bathroom breaks can be handled this way:

"You can only leave this special room when you want to go to the bathroom. We can leave now." *Stating the limit as needed.*

Upon re-entering the room, reintroduce the child to the situation;

"We are in the special room again."

Tip: The bathroom trip can be avoided by structuring the situation before the session begins by simply asking the child if she needs to go to the bathroom prior to entering the playroom.

2. State the limit to the child (level 1):

a. Be succinct and clear.

b. Phrase the limit in a forceful but pleasant tone. Change your voice from the acceptance level to one of authority.

c. In this order, catch the child's attention by saying the child's name, reflect his desire to do the prohibited action, then state the limit.

d. Next, give the child an alternative structure (redirect) to allow him to open up again and redirect his own play.

This statement provides the limit and structure without restricting play too much and allowing the child to make a choice.

"Kassim, remember I told you there are some things you cannot do in here. One thing you cannot do is spit on me. You are really mad. I bet you can make a mad face instead of spitting."

e. If the child persists in asking why, reflect his questions and then answer him with a simple reason.

"You want to know why you cannot throw the ball at mirror. It might break. If the mirror breaks, it will be unsafe in here."

3. Warning (level 2):

If the child breaks the limit that you have just set (the second time this occurs in the session), remind her of the first warning, re-establish the limit, and state what will happen if the limit is broken again. A warning is given so that the child knows beforehand what will happen if she breaks the limit and can decide by herself whether she will risk the consequences.

"Kassim, remember what I just said about spitting. You are super angry at me. You can pretend to spit, but if you spit on me again, our time is up for today."

    4.   Enforcement of consequences (level 3):

Restate the rule and follow through with the consequences you warned the child about. This is critical if you want to be taken seriously by the child. Use a firm but pleasant tone. You can stand up immediately or guide the child to the door to help her clearly distinguish your insistence that she leave now because she has broken a limit (see guidelines for closing a session).

"Kassim, you spit at me again, so now our time is up. You are really upset. I'll see you next time."

When limits are set this way, a child will begin to learn that she is responsible for what happens to her. When a child makes a choice to break a limit, after being warned previously, the child knows what the results will be. After children learn you mean what you say by your follow through, you will find that they do not tend to limit out. Children do not want to lose time in the playroom.

For each subsequent session, start at the warning stage (level 2) and progress to enforcement of consequences (level 3) if necessary.

Should you set the limit?

Direction: Determine if you need to set a limit. Circle "Yes" for limits you need to set and "No" for behaviors that do not require a limit. If you need to set a limit, provide a prosocial alternative to the child. You can check your answers in Appendix A.

- Child wants to leave session early YES NO

Alternative: _____

- Child wants to stand on the chair YES NO

Alternative: _____

- Child spanks you YES NO

Alternative: _____

- Child writes on his face with marker YES NO

Alternative: _____

- Child yells swear words YES NO

Alternative: _____

- Child wants to take clothes off YES NO

Alternative: _____

- Child plays with your hair YES NO

Alternative: _____

- Child kisses you YES NO

Alternative: _____

- Child wants to tie you up YES NO

Alternative: _____

- Child brings in toys from home YES NO

Alternative: _____

- Child wants to take home artwork YES NO

Alternative: _____

- Child sucks on baby bottle YES NO

Alternative: _____

- Child shoots at you with toy gun YES NO

Alternative: _____

- Child says nasty things to you YES NO

Alternative: _____

- Child exposes his private parts YES NO

Alternative: _____

How to Close a Play Therapy Session

Because children generally like the experience of play therapy and the play therapist, leaving the session can be a difficult transition. Stability is paramount in the play therapy relationship. Play therapists, therefore, need to close the session in a consistent and easily recognizable fashion.

Give two time warnings at the session's end. One time warning is to be given at five minutes before the end of the play time:

"Josefina, there are 5 minutes of play time left today."

The last warning is to be given at one minute before the end of session:

"Josefina, we have one more minute left today"

At the end of the session, say firmly, but pleasantly:

"Josefina, our time is up for today. We have to leave now."

Tip: Use the child's name when giving time limits to ground the child in the here and now. Additionally, saying the child's name gets her attention.

Resistance: If the child is reluctant to leave the room, reflect her feelings and restate that the session is ending. Use your body and voice to stress your message.

1. Stand straight up from your physical position at the child's level to your typical adult stance.

2. If there is a light on, turn it off.

3. Go directly to the door and open it.

4. Change the tone of your voice from acceptance to a firm and clear intention.

5. Take the child gently by the back of the shoulder and guide the child in the direction of the door.

6. Explain to the child that for every extra minute she stays, she will lose a minute from the next time.

7. After 5 minutes explain to the child that if she doesn't leave with you now, she cannot come next time.

> Tip: Remember first to reflect the child's feelings before attempting to enforce her leaving.

Structuring the Play Therapy Session: The Cookbook Version

This page is included to ground you in the structuring needed to conduct a play therapy session.

Opening: __name__ this is very special room. You can do *almost* anything in here. If there is something you can't do, I will tell you. You can also say anything.

Limit Setting:

Level 1: __name__ remember I told you there are some things you cannot do in here. One thing you cannot do is _____.

Reflect.

Redirect.

> Example: Stacey, remember, I told you there are some things you cannot do in here. One thing you cannot do is put paint on my face. You really want me to know how messy that feels. You can put paint on my hands or on the doll.

Level 2: ___name___ , remember before I told you that you could not

_____ . If you _____ again, our

session will be over for today.

Reflect.

Redirect.

> Example: <u>Stacey,</u> remember before I told you that you
> could not <u>put paint</u> <u>on my face</u>. If you <u>put paint on my face</u>
> again, our session will be over for today. You're mad that I will
> not let you put the wet, sticky paint on me. You can make my
> hands as yucky as you want.

Level 3: ___name___ our session is over for today.

Reflect.

Repeat (if necessary).

> Example: <u>Stacey</u> our session is over for today. You hate
> that you have to go. <u>Stacey</u> our session is over for today. I will
> see you next time.

Time: ___name___ you have *5 minutes* left today.

Reflect.

___name___ you have *1 minute* left today.

Reflect.

Closing: ___name___ our session is over for today. I'll see you next time.

Reflect.

Themes

Children will demonstrate their perspective of the world in their play. Children may use different toys or behaviors to demonstrate the saliency of their issues. Play therapists are alert to recurring themes in children's play within each session and throughout treatment. Some common themes in children's play are:

ANGER

Themes of anger emerge in many kinds of play. Often children will demonstrate this theme in role plays where they illuminate the dynamics between characters.

POWER/CONTROL

I believe I will see this theme emerge at some point in every child's play because children in dominant U.S. culture are afforded few opportunities for either power or control. This theme is often obvious as the child demonstrates it through the relationship with you.

GRIEF/LOSS

Children (like adults) experience tangible and intangible, death and non-death losses (Fiorini & Mullen, 2006). Themes of loss are therefore incredibly common in children's play. Children share grief and loss themes around losses as divergent as losing a tooth, moving, death, and military deployment of a parent.

TRUST/BETRAYAL/BOUNDARIES

Children referred for therapy are often responding to circumstances of trust and betrayal. Play therapists can anticipate seeing this theme in the play of many children in play therapy. It is likely to emerge even in the first session as the child is unsure about trusting the play therapist.

FEAR

The world can be a very scary place for children. The culture of adulthood does a fine job creating and supporting childhood fears. For example, when my own children indicate being afraid of monsters I usually say something that illuminates this perspective: "Monsters are things grown-ups make up to scare children." Children will show you their fears and also want you to be afraid.

PROTECTION/SAFETY/BOUNDARIES

Protection, safety and boundaries are precarious for many of the children who find their way into the therapeutic playroom. This theme is frequently demonstrated as children experiment with what it would be like to be safe and/or protected.

SELF-ESTEEM

Some children demonstrate so effectively through their play how they feel about themselves. These children often share the perspective of self-esteem through competency play.

ATTENTION

Children need attention - it's how they gain significance (Kottman, 2003). Because many children's needs for attention go unmet, you can expect that they will crop up in the playroom. Verbal cues for this theme are evident when the child says "Look" or "Watch."

OVERWHELMED/CHAOS

Children can get stressed out and overwhelmed. Many children are in circumstances where they have no stability and the adults in their life offer little consistency. These children are likely to be overwhelmed. They demonstrate feeling overwhelmed in the playroom. Their play is chaotic or they create an overwhelming mess to give the play therapist a sense of their experience.

LOYALTY

It's difficult for children to grapple with issues of loyalty. This theme is present in the play of children in the foster care system, as well as children who are in the middle of custody disputes. In their session, they play out the simultaneous pushes and pulls they experience.

CONFUSION

The world and relationships are particularly confusing to children. There are so many mixed messages sent to children that they are likely to try and work out some of their confusion in play therapy sessions. Here's an example: A client of mine, Jonathon, eight years old, entered the playroom and said, "Jodi, I don't get it, how come I cannot hit my brother?" I reflected, "It's confusing to you why that would not be okay." Jonathon replied, "No that's not it. Why can't I hit my brother, but my mom can hit me?"

NURTURANCE

Regression, caretaking and medical play can be characteristic of the play of children expressing this theme.

PERFECTION

Children who have the theme of perfection in their sessions can feel uptight in the playroom. They sometimes get annoyed when things are not exactly as they were in the previous session.

GUILT

Themes of guilt emerge from children's play in play therapy as well. When guilt is the theme, I listen for key words like "Sorry" or play that demonstrates feeling badly after the consequence of actions manifest.

This is not a conclusive list of themes. Themes can sometimes be discerned if the play therapist can think of a title for the session or series of sessions. Teasing out the themes helps with case conceptualization and allows the play therapist to talk respectfully and knowledgably about the child without disclosing specifics with other stakeholders in the child's life.

Firsts

Children move at their own pace in Child-Centered Play Therapy. Adults often perceive the pace of children to be painfully slow. However, play therapists are aware of "firsts" evident in the play therapy session. Firsts are demonstrations of growth and change, and are often pro-social in nature. It behooves play therapists (and their child clients) to share firsts with other supportive adults in the child's life like parents and teachers. The following is a list of common firsts or signs of growth.

In session the child _____ for the first time.

- used play therapist's name
- demonstrated manners (i.e. said please, thank you, excuse me)
- asked for help or didn't ask for help
- left the room at the end of session without incident
- limited her own behavior
- made eye contact
- smiled, laughed, hummed
- verbalized
- used feeling word(s)
- used word(s) that the therapist has used previously
- included the play therapist in her play

NO NOS

In this section I will address the use of questions, praise, and self disclosure from several different perspectives. First I will talk about why I do not want you to use questions in your communications with children in Child-Centered Play Therapy. This will include the use of taggers and a discussion about the role that your confidence plays in turning fine listening responses like tracking and reflections, into responses that are not favorable in Child- Centered Play Therapy, namely questions. I will also talk about the questioning technique commonly referred to as the "whisper technique" (Kottoman, 2001) and how this is relevant to role playing. Additionally, I will address what to do when children ask you questions.

In many adult interactions with children, praise is a component. People use praise with children to help build children's self-esteem. If you observe how adults use praise responses with children, you will likely observe many instances of empty or disingenuous praise. Because children are listening to our verbal communication and are even more in tune with our non- verbal communications, vocal tone, and inflections, they are aware of adults who are praising from a sincere versus insincere place. In Child-Centered Play Therapy you are going to leave praise altogether out of your response repertoire.

It also does not make sense to use self disclosure in Child-Centered Play Therapy sessions. If you are focusing on the child's perspective and phenomenological world, there is no reason for self disclosure. Additionally, children do not gain much from adult self-disclosures because children are egocentric. As much as children love me as their play therapist, they do not need me to change the agenda (and change the focus to me through self-disclosure). Tiffany taught me this concept. Tiffany had just had surgery. She missed a month of play therapy. Upon re-engaging I said, "Welcome back, I bet having your tonsils out hurt." She said, "I feel better." I responded, "I never had my tonsils out." Tiffany replied, "I don't care." Lesson learned: self-disclosure is not consistent with the Child-Centered model.

There a few exercises in this section that should help you become better grounded in these important skills.

NO Questions

When I am training play therapists (and other mental health professionals for that matter) I start with a rule that I hold my students and supervisees to without wavering. There are to be NO questions asked. The rationale behind this is that I believe in order to learn to listen effectively, you need to eliminate questions from the mental health professional's clinical response repertoire. Questions are typically asked from the perspective of the clinician, as Axline (1969), reinforced when she suggested that when the play therapist needs to know why rapport is compromised. Therefore, questions are not appropriate from the Child-Centered perspective because they do not coincide with the Eight Basic Principles. Once the play therapist has asked a question, the child is no longer leading the session, and the play therapist is now the leader. Furthermore, questions tend to rush the process of therapy which is also counter to the Eight Basic Principles. Patience is the key skill in NOT asking questions. If you are patient, you will find that most of your questions will get answered. I truly ask only two questions in Child- Centered Play Therapy; 1) Do you need to go to the bathroom? 2) Do you need a tissue for that?

When you first start using reflections of feeling and tracking statements as responses, you may feel unnatural or robotic. Practice will help, and confidence in your reflective listening skills will come with that practice. Until you gain the confidence that comes with time, proper training, and supervision, you are likely to make tracking and reflective responses that sound like questions because of your inflection at the end of the statement. So a solid reflection like "You are really angry" will come out sounding like a question "You are really angry?" Be patient with yourself and do what it takes to become more confident about your skills. This type of questioning will pass in time.

One more thing… Please promise me that you will never ask a child, "How does that make you feel?" or "Why…" I do not want you to ask any questions in play therapy, but the two aforementioned questions really make me want to scream. Let me tell you why… First of all, you will not need to ask, "How does that make you feel" because you will be observing the child and endeavoring to understand her phenomenological perspective so that you can reflect the feeling with accuracy. In the instances when you are inaccurate, some very cool things happen: 1) the child can correct you if you have created an atmosphere where he feels safe, and 2) you can demonstrate to the child that you can be wrong and still accept yourself.

Additionally, children do not have a large affective adjective vocabulary to draw from in order to answer questions (although their feeling vocabularies will increase as a consequence of routinely having their feelings reflected back to them in Child-Centered Play Therapy). Next there are "Why" questions. "Why" questions tend to put people, including children, on the defensive. In Child- Centered Play Therapy, you want children to feel safe and not like they need to defend. Finally, "why" questions are relatively unanswerable to children who have not yet reached particular milestones in cognitive development. So don't ask questions because they will get in your way of listening and sticking to the Eight Basic Principles and PLEASE, do not ask the questions discussed in this section because, well frankly, they are awful questions!

Exercise 1

Directions: In the exercise that follows please change these commonly asked questions into listening responses. Sample answers can be found in Appendix A.

Example: And how does that make you feel? <u>You are not sure how you are feeling.</u>

1. Why did you do that? _____
2. What could you have done differently? _____
3. How would you like to change this? _____
4. Why do you think that happened? _____
5. Do you want me to color with you? _____

When you need clarification in role plays it is okay to use the "whisper technique" (Kottman, 2001). The whisper technique is a strategy the play therapist uses to gain clarification from the child. For example, the child might say, "Okay, you be the Dad." The therapist can reply in a whisper voice that demonstrates to the child that the play therapist is taking on a different role with the child, "What kind of dad do you want me to be?" These questions can often be avoided by being patient and letting the role play emerge. Another tip with regard to role plays… role-playing takes precedence over responding. If a child includes and directs you in a role play, it is your job to follow their lead and stay in the role. More advanced and seasoned play therapists can often make listening responses while in role; however, until you get to that point through additional training and supervision, stick to following the child's lead and directives.

What's a tagger and why am I avoiding it...

A tagger is the little question we add to the end of a statement that changes a statement into a question. Here's an example to illustrate what I am talking about. "Leah, it's time for bed, *okay?*" or "You understand what I am saying about why you should not ask questions, *right?*" It is typical to use taggers in everyday speech. Listen to the people around you (yourself included) and you will be amazed at how frequently taggers are used. You need to be very careful about letting these critters sneak into your speech in play therapy because children are like little lawyers and will find the loopholes in your statements. Here's an example of a critical time when a tagger would get in the way: "Andrew, our session is over for today, *okay?"* Andrew could say "No" as if you asked him a question, which by including a tagger you actually just did. A potential power struggle could emerge making it unpleasant for both you and Andrew, which could jeopardize your relationship. It may be very difficult to rid yourself of these nasty taggers at first. There are several reasons why they are so difficult to remove from your speech: 1) they are ingrained. If you are part of a marginalized or devalued group culturally, you have been socialized to be unsure of yourself and will likely use taggers with relative consistency and frequency, and 2) when you are feeling unsure or lacking confidence, which I anticipate you might be when you begin doing play therapy, you are likely to demonstrate your lack of confidence by including taggers in your speech. I would like you to work hard on eliminating taggers from your speech, *you know what I mean?*

NO Answers to Questions (within reason)

Children will be very curious about you, the play therapy process, playroom and toys. You can anticipate that they will, therefore, ask you questions. Additionally, some children use question asking to form or conversely, to avoid relationships. In Child-Centered Play Therapy, in order to stay grounded in the philosophy and Eight Basic Principles, it is best to try and reflect the child's feeling when asked a question. Usually, if you use a reflection to respond to the question, you have met the child's need and she moves on. Sometimes the child persists and asks again. Try reflecting again. In the event that this does not work and the question is an answerable question, then answer the question. It has been my experience that once I answer one question, the child asks many more. These questions seem to get in the way of my relationship with the child.

Here's an example of what typically happens (and what typically happens is that the child moves on).

Child "What's this toy?"

PT: "You are wondering what that's supposed to be?"

Child "It's a boat."

PT: "You are confident you know what it is."

With a more persistent child

Child: "How much more time is left?"

PT: "You are worried we are running out of time."

Child: "Yes, how much time is left?"

PT: "You would feel more comfortable if you knew how much time was left."

Child: "Yeah."

With an even more persistent child

Child: "How old are you?"

PT: "You are wondering about me."

Child: "Yeah, how old are you?"

PT: "You are very curious."

Child: "Just tell me."

PT: 36

One quick story before you practice this skill…

Several years ago I worked with an intellectually delayed 12-year-old boy named Chris. Chris was well-suited for Child-Centered Play Therapy and responded very well to the approach. However, Chris would ask me many questions during our time together. I gathered that this was his way of demonstrating to me that he cared about me. A typical exchange would go something like this:

Chris: "How old are you?"

Jodi: "You are curious about me."

Chris: "Do you have kids?"

Jodi: "You are wondering what I do when I am not in here with you."

Chris: "What did you eat for dinner last night?"

Jodi: "You want to tell me about what you like to eat."

This could go on for the entire session. The incessant question asking did not stand in the way of his playing so I was usually able to break up the responses to his questions with responses gleaned from his play and facial expressions. One day I decided to see what would happen if I just answered. I had known Chris long enough to know that he would not stick with the same question if I reflected, and would simply pick another question. Here's what happened:

Chris: "What's your Dad's name?" Jodi: "Marty."

Chris: "Tell him I say Hi!"

And that was it. No more questions for the entire session!

This is not an example of a solid Child-Centered Play Therapy interchange, although it is a good story, *don't you think?* (Yes, that is a tagger.)

Exercise 2

Directions: Respond to the child's query with a reflection (see examples in the above discussion).

The following are all questions either myself or my supervisees have been asked.

1. What time is it? _____

2. Do other kids come here?_____

3. Do you have kids? _____

4. What's this toy called? _____

5. Why do you talk like that?_____

6. Can I swear in here? _____

7. Can I stay more minutes?_____

8. Why can't I spank you? _____

9. Do you love me? _____

10. Can I leave now? _____

Exercise 3

Challenge questions:

1. Are you a boy or a girl? _____

2. How come you're so fat?_____

3. Would you like to see my penis? _____

4. You're breath smells, what did you eat for lunch?

   _____

5. Do you want to smell my fart? _____

NO Praise

You may be shocked to learn that praise is not an acceptable response to children in an approach where children are valued, honored and respected. In fact, that is exactly why praise is not used. When praise is used as a response, the praiser is communicating his or her perspective. In Child- Centered Play Therapy the focus is on the perspective of the child.

Here's an example to illustrate this point:

> Taylor: "I did it. I made a basket"
> Praiser: "I am so proud of you."

In this example the child's esteem is connected to the praiser. Without the praiser and the praise, there is no connection to the esteem. The praise and esteem are located outside of the child. The child does not own the positive perspective of self. Observe the subtle, but critical differences in the example that follows.

> Taylor: "I did it. I made a basket"
> Play Therapist: "You are so proud and excited."

In this example the child's perspective of self is recognized. The child owns the feelings of pride. The pride is located inside of the child where it can be accessed at any time, not only in the presence of the praiser.

It will be very difficult for some of you to leave praise outside of the play therapy relationship. If you follow the Child-Centered approach, you will need to do just that.

Although praise is "nice," it is still a judgment. Child-Centered play therapists do not stand in judgment of their clients.

In the following exercise there are examples of interactions with children that often elicit praise responses. Please correct the praise response with a response that demonstrates an understanding of the child's perspective, using either reflections of feeling or tracking responses. Refer to the above discussion for examples. Sample answers can be found in Appendix A.

1. Greg: "I did it. Do you like it?"

Praiser: "I am so proud of you. It's awesome."

Therapist: _____

2. Jaielle: : "Here catch"

Praiser: "That was a good throw."

Therapist: _____

3. Tiki: "Look how tall I made the building."

Praiser: "Wow, you did a great job."

Therapist: _____

4. Juanita: (Puts on princess crown). "I am the fairest in the land."

Praiser: "You look beautiful."

Therapist: _____

5. Griffin: (Draws a picture, looks at you and smiles)

Praiser: "That's a terrific picture."

Therapist: _____

READY FOR PRACTICE (AND PLAY)

This section contains discussion and exercises to ready you for the practice of play therapy. I want to again remind you here that this workbook is not a substitute for training and supervision. This workbook is designed to augment training and supervision through reinforcing skills and providing multiple ways of learning the philosophy and the approach.

In this section, I will cover some of the typical worries of beginning play therapists, like termination issues and the progression of a child's play. I will also share with you the questions my students and supervisees typically ask as they prepare for their very first play therapy session. It is difficult to judge your effectiveness in the early stages of your development as a play therapist. You will complete an exercise designed to help you assess the impact of the responses you are making in play therapy. I have also included a comprehensive list of treatment plan goals that are consistent with the Child-Centered approach. The impetus for the creation and inclusion of this information comes directly from the mental health field. Many of my supervisees struggle with having to fit the Child-Centered approach into agency-based paperwork and documentation designed specifically for other approaches to counseling children. I hope you find this a useful inclusion. Lastly, you will find a unique overview of the benefits of Child-Centered Play Therapy described from an adult-imagined perspective of the child. This is included to help center you as you embark into the magical relationship that is achieved through the Child-Centered Play Therapy approach.

Stages of Child-Centered Play Therapy

In general, children involved in Child-Centered Play Therapy will progress through stages. There is no prescribed length of time for any of these stages, as children move at their own pace.

Stage 1: **Warm-up**

This stage of therapy is characterized by the forming of the relationship. The child may ask a considerable amount of questions during this time. The child may also test the therapist. Can I really do just about anything in here? Can I really say anything? This stage may last up to two months. This warm-up stage will be longer for children with attachment difficulties or loss histories characterized by abandonment and betrayal.

Stage 2: **Aggression and Pain**

Children will demonstrate their anger and pain during this stage and it can be intense. Their perceptions may not match the reality of what happened. However, children's perceptions will match their affective reality.

Stage 3: **Dependence and Independence**

The child in this stage will want you to do or not do for him. Children will test their independence and dependence. The therapist should not do for the child what the child can do for himself.

Stage 4: **Mastery**

This is typically the final stage of therapy. There will be a change in play (see termination information). Children will consistently demonstrate competency in this stage. Their play will be playful. The child will demonstrate socially appropriate behaviors in and out of the play therapy sessions.

Stage 5: **Relationship Building**

In this stage the child may return to testing the relationship. She may show fear and confusion about the pending termination of the relationship. The child needs to know that even though you will no longer be seeing her in therapy, this is an important relationship.

Adapted from: Nordling, W. J., & Guerney, L. (1999). Typical stages in Child-Centered play therapy process. *The Journal for Professional Counselor, 14(1), 17-23.*

Is the Child Ready for Termination?

Determining when it is time for termination in Child-Centered Play Therapy is a difficult task. Accurate determination requires that the therapist has paid close attention to themes and firsts. A child who is ready for termination will no longer display themes that were evident previously in therapy and the child will consistently demonstrate prosocial firsts. The child may seem bored, may leave the session before their time has run out and the child may even say, "I don't want to come see you anymore." Child- Centered Play Therapy is Child-Centered to the end ideally. Some changes in the child to consider are:

- Child is less dependent.
- Child is less confused.
- Child expresses needs openly.
- Child is able to focus on self.
- Child accepts responsibility for own actions and feelings.
- Child limits own behavior appropriately.
- Child is more inner directed.
- Child is less rigid.
- Child is consistently demonstrating pro-social behavior outside of sessions.
- Child is more tolerant of the unpredictability of life.
- Child initiates activities with assurance and confidence.
- Child is cooperative but not conforming.
- Child expresses anger appropriately, pro-socially.
- Child is consistently in a relatively good mood.
- Child is more accepting of self even when she makes mistakes.
- Child is able to play out story sequences, the play has direction, and makes sense.
- Child's play has light-heartedness about it; the play is playful.

Adapted from: Landreth, G. (2002). *Play therapy: The art of the relationship (2nd ed.)*. New York: Brunner-Routledge.

What about...Commonly asked questions about the practice of Play Therapy

Directions: Attempt to answer each question on your own. Answers and discussion can be found in the answer key in Appendix A.

1. What if the child will not talk?
2. What if the child wants to bring in a friend, parent, sibling?

3. What about sand, paint, water, MESSES?

4. What do you do when the child won't leave the playroom?

5. What about swearing, cussing, hate language?

6. What about having toy guns in the playroom?

7. What if the child wants to leave the session early?

8. What about settings where noise in the playroom is a factor to others in close proximity?

9. What if the child is being rude to the play therapist?

10. What if the child tells others she can use bad words in session?

11. What about children putting toys in their mouths?

12. What about children breaking toys?

13. What if they want to bring in a toy from home?

14. What about interruptions from others during play therapy sessions?

15. What if a child discloses abuse during a session?

16. What if a child doesn't feel well and does not want to play or participate?

17. How can play therapists honor diversity?

18. What do you do when a child tells you they love you?

19. What should you do if the child-client falls asleep in session?

Evaluating the Impact of the Play Therapist's Responses

The play therapist should be able to assess the ongoing impact of his responses to the child. It is the play therapist's responsibility to ascertain when responses are accurate, inaccurate, therapeutic, non- therapeutic, tolerable, and/or threatening to the child.

What do the following actions suggest about the play therapist's responses to the child? Check all that apply. Answers and discussion can be found in Appendix A.

Behavior	Accurate	Inaccurate	Therapeutic	Non-Therapeutic	Tolerable	Threatening
1. Child moves closer to play therapist.						
2. Child moves away from play therapist.						
3. Play intensifies.						
4. Child uses play therapist's words.						
5. Child corrects play therapist.						
6. Child turns away from play therapist.						
7. Child invites play therapist into play.						
8. Child tells play therapist to shut up, stop talking.						
9. Child nods "yes" after response.						
10. Child wants to end session.						
11. Child's play changes abruptly.						
12. Child's play is additive.						
13. Child smiles.						
14. Child looks at the play therapist.						
15. Child ignores the play therapist.						

Child-Centered Play Therapy Implementation Checklist

This is a brief version of the *Child-Centered Play Therapy Implementation Checklist* (Mullen & Uninsky, 2007). After completing the workbook it may be helpful to use the rating form as a tool to gauge your adherence to the Child-Centered Play Therapy model. It would be appropriate to share this information in peer or clinical supervision contexts as you begin to integrate what you have learned.

Program Area/Quality Indicator	Final Rating: Level of Strategy Implementation				
1. Introducing the CCPT Project					
Implementation Indicator 1.1: Building Rapport with the client: The therapist establishes a trusting relationship with the participating child.	c None	d Minimal	e Moderate	f Complete	g Exemplary
Implementation Indicator 1.2: Assuring confidentiality: The therapist successfully assures the parent(s) or caregiver(s) that all information disclosed will be kept strictly confidential. The therapist also assures the participating client, but only if s/he is capable of understanding the issues related to confidentiality.	c None	d Minimal	e Moderate	f Complete	g Exemplary
Implementation Indicator 1.3: Gathering background information: The therapist collects information in a comprehensive manner to permit a thorough understanding of the phenomenological perspective of the child.	c None	d Minimal	e Moderate	f Complete	g Exemplary
Implementation Indicator 1.4: Orienting to the program: The therapist provides an introduction to Child-Centered Play Therapy, highlighting the key features and articulating the expected course of the intervention.	c None	d Minimal	e Moderate	f Complete	g Exemplary
Implementation Indicator 1.5: Encouraging involvement: The therapist uses a variety of techniques (including the use of toys) to facilitate child involvement, play and verbalizations.	c None	d Minimal	e Moderate	f Complete	g Exemplary
Implementation Indicator 1.6: Developing and using an appropriate play therapy environment: The therapist introduces and uses appropriate playroom materials.	c None	d Minimal	e Moderate	f Complete	g Exemplary

Program Area/Quality Indicator	Final Rating: Level of Strategy Implementation				
2. Treatment					
Implementation Indicator 2.1: Structuring the relationship: The therapist introduces the parameters and nature of the play therapy relationship.	c None	d Minimal	e Moderate	f Complete	g Exemplary
Implementation Indicator 2.2: Acknowledging the culture of children: The therapist acknowledges and demonstrates appreciation of the developmental and socio-cultural perspectives of the child.	c None	d Minimal	e Moderate	f Complete	g Exemplary
Implementation Indicator 2.3: Role-play to identify feelings, and behaviors: The therapist and the child engage in role-play to help the child identify feelings and behaviors.	c None	d Minimal	e Moderate	f Complete	g Exemplary
Implementation Indicator 2.4: Establishing limits: The therapist sets limits, as needed, to provide additional structure to sessions and to maintain safety.	c None	d Minimal	e Moderate	f Complete	g Exemplary
Implementation Indicator 2.5: Therapeutic responses: The therapist provides ongoing responses calibrated to help the child in feeling understood, in becoming aware of his/her responsibility in the therapeutic relationship, and in gaining insight into his/her behavior.	c None	d Minimal	e Moderate	f Complete	g Exemplary
Implementation Indicator 2.6: Role-playing and play to improve coping skills: The therapist and the child act out scenarios to provide an opportunity for the child to practice coping skills and to utilize a problem-solving approach to difficult situations.	c None	d Minimal	e Moderate	f Complete	g Exemplary
Implementation Indicator 2.7: Outcome indicators for clients with family problems: When family problems are diagnosed, the therapist works to establish a range of outcomes intended to improve, where needed, the child's communication, relational, and coping skills.	c None	d Minimal	e Moderate	f Complete	g Exemplary
Implementation Indicator 2.8: Outcome indicators for clients with educational problems: When educational problems are indicated, the therapist works to establish a range of outcomes intended to improve, where needed, the child's communication, relational, and coping skills.	c None	d Minimal	e Moderate	f Complete	g Exemplary
Implementation Indicator 2.9: Outcome indicators for clients with mental health problems: When mental health problems are diagnosed, the therapist works to establish a range of outcomes intended to improve, where needed, the child's social and emotional coping skills.	c None	d Minimal	e Moderate	f Complete	g Exemplary

Example Treatment Plan Goals Consistent with Child-Centered Play Therapy

Family Problems

- Child will demonstrate improved communication skills with parents.
- Child will demonstrate improved communication skills with siblings.
- Child will demonstrate improved communication skills with extended family members.
- Child will demonstrate improved relational skills with parents.
- Child will demonstrate improved relational skills with siblings.
- Child will demonstrate improved relational skills with extended family members.
- Child will be able to communicate feelings in a developmentally appropriate fashion.
- Child will respect boundaries and limits set by family members within normal limits for age and developmental ability.
- Child will demonstrate pro-social skills.
- Child will demonstrate problem-solving skills.

Educational Problems

- Child will demonstrate improved communication skills with teachers and educational staff.
- Child will demonstrate improved communication skills with peers.
- Child will demonstrate improved relational skills with teachers and educational staff.
- Child will demonstrate improved relational skills with peers.
- Child will respect boundaries and limits set by teachers and educational staff within normal limits for age and developmental ability.
- Child will respect boundaries and limits set by peers within normal limits for age and developmental ability.
- Child will use time in play therapy to demonstrate aggression, regression, and expression that is not appropriate for the classroom.

- Child will demonstrate pro-social skills.
- Child will demonstrate problem-solving skills.
- Child will emotionally contain in the classroom.
- Child will seek appropriate support services in the school.

Mental Health Problems

- Child will engage in the play therapy process.
- Child will respect boundaries and limits set by the play therapist.
- Child will begin to express feelings verbally.
- Child's acting out (anger, depression, anxiety) behavior will abate.
- Child will be able to demonstrate insight.
- Child will be able to set culturally appropriate boundaries.
- Child will use play therapy sessions to explore mental health issues.
- Child's mood will stabilize.
- Child will share his or her perspective of the experience of trauma.
- Child will make pro-social choices.
- Child will demonstrate emotional problem solving.
- Child will smile and laugh at appropriate times.
- Child's mood and affect will be congruent.
- Child will express a complex variety of feelings.

PERMISSION: The Gift of Child-Centered Play Therapy

Permission to be different.

Permission to discover, appreciate, and develop their inner selves.

Permission to make mistakes. Permission to learn from their mistakes. Permission to move at their own pace. Permission to direct their own behavior. Permission to make choices.

Permission to self-discipline. Permission to self-correct.

Permission to experience negative emotions.

Permission to feel.

Permission to have a warm, trusting relationship with an adult.

Permission to tell their story in their own way.

Permission to love.

Permission to test out who they want to be.

Permission to make things up. Permission to achieve success. Permission to manage their emotion. Permission to be cooperative. Permission to say no.

Permission to resist authority.

Permission to be a child. Permission to be quiet. Permission to cry. Permission to be a baby.

Permission to feel sorry for self.

Permission to think. Permission to show anger. Permission to hate. Permission to be yourself.

Permission to hear the acceptance of another.

Permission to have a self. Permission to fear and be afraid. Permission to withdraw.

Permission to pretend.

Permission to learn from yourself. Permission to comfort yourself. Permission to trust an adult. Permission to trust yourself. Permission to be.

Permission to Play.

Dear Play Therapy

Writing a letter to "Play Therapy"

Whew! You have made it to the relative end of this workbook.

As I stated in the Introduction, working with children isn't for everyone, doing play therapy isn't for everyone, practicing Child-Centered Play Therapy isn't for everyone. The skills consistent with this approach will be valuable in your relationships, both personal and professional, with children and adults. You do not have to be a Child-Centered play therapist to be respectful and thoughtful in your relationships. I am certain that we are all capable of that. Many of you, however, will realize that this makes sense for you and this is how you want to work clinically with children. Remember, to do this work, this way, you have to embrace the philosophy. If you don't believe in the philosophy of Child Centered Play Therapy, you will never be able to fake your way through the approach, so please do not try.

Ok, so if you think you have found what you've been looking for, there are two things I need you to do.

1. Get training and supervision. It's out there and you don't have to look far. Check out The Association for Play Therapy's web site: www.a4pt.org. I am committed to the preparation of play therapists, so if you cannot find training or supervision contacts, find me at www.integrativecounseling.us.

2. Write a letter. No, not just any letter…I want you to write a letter to play therapy. Write it as if "Play Therapy" had human qualities (Mullen, 2003b).

Dear Play Therapy: _____

_____

_____

_____

_____

_____

_____

_____

_____

_____

_____

_____

_____

_____

_____

_____

After you have written your letter, read it to a supportive person in your life who will be excited about what you have learned for no other reason except that you are excited. If you do not have that person in your life at this moment, I would be honored for you to share your letter with me.

Here's my latest letter…

Dear Play Therapy:

Yes, it's me again. Well I have so much I want to share with you and yet I feel limited by words.

I know you of all people understand that! I guess I really just want to say thank you, again. I feel so blessed to have you in my life. Because of you I have made connections to people who I cannot imagine otherwise connecting with. It is an honor and responsibility. I realize daily, both aspects of that gift.

I thank you for sharing with me your simple secrets which have provided me with passion. I cannot seem to get enough of you. Case in point I am writing you this letter at 2:30am.

Well I don't want to go on and on, and you know I could, I just want to say thank you. Thank you for being the motivation for me to be the best professional counselor, counselor educator, supervisor, parent and person I can be.

Love you, Jodi

Here's a letter to play therapy from a budding play therapist Yuka Maruyama.

Dear Play Therapy, How are you?

I can't believe that it's been over one and a half years since I got to know you.

When I was in Japan, I was kind of interested in you, but couldn't get much information about you. I didn't think I would get close to you this much when Jenn introduced me to you.

I think I really like you, and you like me too. I can be myself when I'm with you. But sometimes you make me nervous because there are still many things I don't know and need to know about you.

The other day, I talked with Hayashi-sensei about you. She said that Japanese government tried to make you popular (because of school problems and abuse problems) but there are not many people who really know you. You know, there are some people who "pretend" they know you. So, I think I wanna make you a big star when I go back to Japan. If I can get the opportunity to stay in the states and learn more about you...

You will be my life partner, if you really like me -

Sincerely, Yuka

Pathways to Advanced Training and Credentialing in Play Therapy

National Institute for Relationship Enhancement (NIRE) Certification in Play Therapy

This program leads to certification in Child-Centered play therapy.

Credential earned: CCPT (Child-Centered Play Therapist)

Credential of Supervisor: CCPT-S (Child-Centered Play Therapist Supervisor)

Program Requirements: In order to enroll in the program individuals must submit an application, have an earned master's degree in a helping profession OR be currently matriculated in such a program, and have a three credit graduate level course in play therapy or the equivalent in workshops.

Parameters of the program: Supervisees submit recorded sessions for review by a supervisor. Supervisees will earn a minimum of 26 hours of clinical supervision. Supervision can be face to face, phone and/or video conference. Individual and group supervision formats are allowed.

Fees: There is an application fee (for the most accurate fee see www.nire.org) and fees for supervision that are set by NIRE, but supervisors are able to set fees independently.

Association for Play Therapy (APT) Certification in Play Therapy

This program leads to certification in play therapy.

Credential earned: RPT (Registered Play Therapist)

Credential of Supervisor: RPT-S (Registered Play Therapist Supervisor)

Program Requirements: In order to enroll in the program individuals must submit an application, have an earned master's degree in a helping profession, hold a license or certification in said helping profession and have a coursework in play therapy (or the equivalent in workshops (150 continuing education hours). See the APT web site for further explanation and clarification (www.a4pt.org).

Parameters of the program: Supervisees will earn a minimum number of continuing education hours in play therapy. Clinical supervision is also necessary and can be face to face and/or phone. Individual and group supervision formats are allowed.

Fees: There is an application fee (for the most accurate fee see www.a4pt.org). Fees for supervision are set by supervisors.

***I encourage interested people to seek credentialing through NIRE **and** APT. The entire NIRE program can be applied to APT credentialing program. In essence, supervisees can pick up the NIRE credential on the way to earning the APT credential. I am credentialed as both a NIRE and APT supervisor. Please feel free to contact me if you need help in negotiating the process. ***

-Jodi Mullen

USEFUL RESOURCES

How to Watch a Play Therapy Session to Optimize Your Learning

One way to keep improving your play therapy skills is to record your sessions and view them through an honest lens. However, watching your sessions can be difficult because often during that time your inner critic gets very loud. Our inner critic notices and exaggerates everything we do that is not perfect. This includes play therapy skills, of course, but is not limited to skills. That inner critic will make fun of you, tell you your clothes don't look good, and pick you apart; anything about you is fair game. Three things to remember: there is no such thing as a perfect play therapy session (or counseling session of any kind for that matter), there is no such thing as a perfect play therapist (think unicorn), and finally, it is not what you do, but *who you are* that truly matters in the therapeutic relationship. Your inner critic can override the voice of your inner coach and inner clinical supervisor so that you don't wind up really benefitting from watching your recorded sessions, especially early on in your practice.

You can circumvent that inner critic and still benefit from viewing recorded play therapy sessions by accessing ones that are available as resources from other play therapy practitioners. You can even find them on social media. To truly optimize the experience of viewing the play therapy session of another practitioner, you have to make it an active rather than passive endeavor. The following questions and tasks are shared with you here as a means of helping you turn the passive process of viewing a recorded play therapy session into an active one.

1. What does this play therapist do well? Be specific. List examples.

2. Record **ALL** the feelings this child expressed. For each feeling word, write a synonym that is developmentally and culturally appropriate for this child.

3. What can this play therapist improve on? Be specific. Give examples.

4. What do you admire about this play therapist? Why?

5. What do you like about this child?

6. Do you notice any themes in this child's play? What are they?

7. Did the play therapist set adequate limits? If not, what was the error and how would you have corrected it?

8. What approach to play therapy is demonstrated in this session? What's the evidence? Give examples.

9. What do you notice about yourself thinking, feeling, sensing, as you watch this person?

10. Think of this child as your play therapy teacher. What lessons did you learn about...

☐ Play therapy?
☐ Children/childhood?
☐ Yourself?

11. What surprised you about this play therapy session?

12. What questions would you like to have answered by a play therapy supervisor or expert related to this session?

Self-Supervision Form for Child-Centered Play Therapy Sessions

Date of Session: _____

Child's Name: _____

Date of Review: _____

Age: _____ Session #: _____

1. List feelings expressed by the child. Put "X" next to feelings you reflected. Put "O" next to feelings you could have reflected.

- ☐ _____
- ☐ _____
- ☐ _____
- ☐ _____
- ☐ _____
- ☐ _____
- ☐ _____
- ☐ _____
- ☐ _____
- ☐ _____
- ☐ _____
- ☐ _____

2. My overall responses to child's feelings. Give examples and evidence.

Were they accurate? Were they complete?
Were they timed appropriately?

3. Which of the child's feelings, if any, did I not respond to appropriately?

4. What kind of error was committed in responding inappropriately? (Give specific examples)

Failure to respond at all.

Failure to respond until much later.

Addressing action instead of feeling.

Mis-labeling of feelings.

Failure to match own degree of emotion with that expressed by child.

5. Frequency of responses. (Give specific examples)

Balanced.

Too few responses made to demonstrate understanding and acceptance of the child.

Too much talking.

Failure to make succinct responses.

Play-by-play description.

Too much interest to unimportant details.

Other?

6. Were limits enforced appropriately?

Too many. (What's the evidence?)

Too few. (How do you know?)

Not enforced? (Why not?)

Other?

7. Was structuring provided appropriately? (How do you know?)

Opening

5 minutes

1 minute

Closing

Was timing appropriate?

8. Was factual information provided appropriately? If not, how was the error made?

Refused to provide any answers, reflecting child's wish for an answer beyond a reasonable point.

Too much information provided, more than required.

Misleading information provided, avoided facing the truth.

9. Proximity

Too close.

Too far away.

Child looked uncomfortable with distance.

Adult looked uncomfortable with distance.

10. Language

Adult uses language appropriate for the child's age and cognitive development.

Give 3 examples.

1. _____

2. _____

3. _____

11. Control of adult's feelings. Give examples.

Adequate.

Own opinions, evaluations, judgments crept in.

Face revealed contradictory feeling.

Voice revealed contradictory feelings.

Appears uninterested, distracted.

12. Adult carries off technique comfortably? If not, what was evidenced to suggest otherwise.

> Adult seems uncomfortable. How?
>
> Child criticizes or rebuffs technique.

13. Adult is comfortable with child's direction of the session. Does not attempt to divert by open or subtle means. If not, explain the error.

14. Apparent themes in the child's play.

15. What did you like about the child?

16. What about this child reminded you of yourself?

17. What's your overall feeling about the session?

18. Most positive aspect of session.

19. Aspects to work on.

20. How was the process of completing this supervision form for you?

21. Additional notes…

Play Therapy Session Clinical Notes

Play Therapy Session Clinical Notes

Client Name:	Date:	Time of session:
Counselor:	Session #	Length of session:

Transitioned into Session: ☐ enthusiastically ☐ wearily ☐ anxiously ☐ irritably ☐ tentatively
☐ excitedly ☐ boastfully ☐ begrudgingly ☐ calmly ☐ inquisitively ☐ merrily ☐ _____
as evidenced by: _____

Toys Used:

☐ Action heroes/soldiers	☐ Cars/trucks	☐ Animals: domestic; zoo; dinosaurs; _____
☐ Bop Bag/egg cartons/socker bopper	☐ Dress up/masks	☐ Water
☐ Baby dolls/bottle	☐ Guns/handcuffs/rope	☐ Camera
☐ Doll house/small figures	☐ Swords/noodles/shields	☐ Puppets
☐ Crayons/markers/whiteboard/paint	☐ Doctor kit	☐ Kitchen/dishes/food
☐ Sand/miniatures	☐ Telephone	☐ Money/cash register
☐ Blocks/legos	☐ Basketball/hoop/balls	☐ _____

Subjective Feelings Expressed:
HAPPY: relieved, satisfied, pleased, delighted, excited, surprised, _____ silly,
SAD: disappointed, hopeless, pessimistic, discouraged, lonely, _____
ANGRY: impatient, annoyed, frustrated, mad, mean, jealous, _____
AFRAID: vulnerable, helpless, distrustful, anxious, fearful, scared, terrified, _____
CONFIDENT: proud, strong, powerful, determined, free, _____
HESITANT: timid, confused, nervous, embarrassed, ashamed, _____
CURIOUS: interested, focused, _____

_____
FLAT: contained, ambiguous, restricted, apathetic, bored _____

Themes:

☐ Relationship: connecting; trust; approval-seeking; manipulative; limit-testing; _____
☐ Mastery: deconstructive; constructive; competency; resolution; integrative; _____
☐ Adjustment/Change
☐ Boundaries/Intrusion   ☐ Power/Control
☐ Dependence/Independence ☐ Exploratory
☐ Helpless/Inadequate   ☐ Loneliness
☐ Aggression/Revenge   ☐ Confusion
☐ Self-Esteem/Self-Worth   ☐ Fears/Anxiety
☐ Safety/Security/Protection   ☐ Good vs. Evil
☐ Nurturing/Self-Care/Healing ☐ Anger/Sadness
☐ Death/Loss/Grieving   ☐ Trust/Betrayal
☐   ☐

Session Narrative include subjective feelings and themes. Significant verbalizations "Firsts," additive or cycling play, description of role play or other content:
_____
_____
_____
_____
_____
_____
_____
_____
_____
_____
_____
_____
_____
_____
_____
_____

Prosocial Behaviors Displayed:
☐ Manners   ☐ Care taking   ☐ Self-control
☐ Sharing   ☐ Respect   ☐ Picking Up
☐ Empathy   ☐ Mutuality   ☐ Apologizing
☐ Problem Solving ☐ _____   ☐ _____

Limits set and response of the child:
_____
_____
_____

Transitioned out of Session: ☐ enthusiastically ☐ excitedly ☐ wearily ☐ anxiously ☐ easily
☐ begrudgingly ☐ boastfully ☐ tentatively ☐ merrily ☐ irritably ☐ calmly ☐ _____
as evidenced by: _____

Reminders/other notes:

Integrative Counseling Services, PLLC & Jodi Ann Mullen, PhD, LMHC, NCC, RPT-S, 2007

Play Therapy Session Clinical Notes

Client Name: Mary-Anne	Date: 6/20/19	Time of session: 1:30pm
Counselor: Jodi	Session # 6	Length of session: 30m

Transitioned into Session: ☐ enthusiastically ☐ wearily ☐ anxiously ☐ irritably ☐ tentatively
☒ excitedly ☐ boastfully ☐ begrudgingly ☐ calmly ☐ inquisitively ☐ merrily ☐ _____
as evidenced by: Smiling and running into the playroom

Toys Used:
☒ Action heroes/soldiers ☒ Cars/trucks ☒ Animals: domestic; zoo; dinosaurs; _____
☐ Bop Bag/egg cartons/socker bopper ☐ Dress up/masks ☐ Water
☐ Baby dolls/bottle ☐ Guns/handcuffs/rope ☐ Camera
☐ Doll house/small figures ☐ Swords/noodles/shields ☐ Puppets
☐ Crayons/markers/whiteboard/paint ☐ Doctor kit ☒ Kitchen/dishes/food
☐ Sand/miniatures ☒ Telephone ☒ Money/cash register
☒ Blocks/legos ☐ Basketball/hoop/balls ☐ _____

Subjective Feelings Expressed:
(HAPPY) relieved, (satisfied,) pleased, delighted, (excited,) (surprised,) silly, _____
SAD: (disappointed,) hopeless, pessimistic, discouraged, lonely, _____
ANGRY: (impatient,) (annoyed,) (frustrated,) mad, mean, jealous, _____
AFRAID: vulnerable, helpless, distrustful, anxious, fearful, scared, terrified, _____
CONFIDENT: (proud,) (strong,) (powerful,) determined, free, _____
HESITANT: timid, confused, nervous, embarrassed, ashamed, _____
CURIOUS: interested (focused.) _____

FLAT: contained, ambiguous, restricted, apathetic, bored _____

Session Narrative include subjective feelings and themes. Significant verbalizations "Firsts," additive or cycling play, description of role play or other content:
The client entered session excitedly, as he smiled and ran into the playroom. He got out the cash register and food and said he needed to buy food for his baby doll. I reflected that he wanted to take care of his baby. Then he began playing with the cars/trucks. There are themes of aggression when laying with the cars. He became frustrated and annoyed when the blocks he was building fell over. When our time was up he stated he did not want to leave.

Themes:
☒ Relationship: (connecting,) (trust;) approval-seeking; manipulative (limit-testing;) _____
☒ Mastery: (deconstructive;) (constructive;) competency; resolution; integrative; _____
☐ Adjustment/Change
☐ Boundaries/Intrusion ☒ Power/Control
☐ Dependence/Independence ☒ Exploratory
☐ Helpless/Inadequate ☐ Loneliness
☒ Aggression/Revenge ☐ Confusion
☐ Self-Esteem/Self-Worth ☐ Fears/Anxiety
☐ Safety/Security/Protection ☐ Good vs. Evil
☒ Nurturing/Self-Care/Healing ☐ Anger/Sadness
☐ Death/Loss/Grieving ☐ Trust/Betrayal
☐ _____ ☐ _____

Prosocial Behaviors Displayed:
☒ Manners ☒ Caretaking ☐ Self-control
☒ Sharing ☒ Respect ☒ Picking Up
☐ Empathy ☒ Mutuality ☐ Apologizing
☒ Problem Solving ☐ _____ ☐ _____

Limits set and response of the child: _I let the client know he could not throw the ball at my face, he was O.K. with this and did not do it again._____

Transitioned out of Session: ☐ enthusiastically ☐ excitedly ☐ wearily ☐ anxiously ☐ inquisitively
☐ begrudgingly ☐ boastfully ☐ tentatively ☐ merrily ☒ irritably ☐ calmly ☐ _____
as evidenced by: __Saying, "Ugh, I don't want to leave"

Reminders/other notes:

Weekly Parent Report (optional)

Date: _____

Counselor: _____

Child's Name: _____

Parent's Name: _____

1. Has anything significant happened in your child's life since last session (positive or negative) i.e. family, school, sleeping, friends, health, etc.

2.   Assessment of Changes in Child

Child's overall behavior compared to last time:

1	2	3	4	5	6	7	8	9	10
Not as good				Same					Better

Child's concerning behavior	Compared to last time (circle one)	Additional Note
	Not as good Same Better	
	Not as good Same Better	
	Not as good Same Better	
	Not as good Same Better	
	Not as good Same Better	

Child's mood/attitude towards life, compared to last time:

1	2	3	4	5	6	7	8	9	10
Not as good				Same					Better

My experience parenting my child compared to last time:

1	2	3	4	5	6	7	8	9	10
Not as good				Same					Better

What methods did you try?

Method	How did your child respond?	Would you do anything differently?

☐ **It's very important that I speak with you as soon as possible.**

☐ **I need to talk with you before next time you come. (Note: Counselors are not always available to talk after each session.)**

_____

_____

_____

_____

_____

_____

_____

_____

_____

_____

_____

_____

_____

_____

_____

_____

_____

_____

Weekly Teacher Report (optional)

Date: _____

Counselor: _____

Child's Name: _____

Teacher's Name: _____

1.Has anything significant happened in your student's life since last session (positive or negative) i.e. family, school, friends, health, etc.

2.   Assessment of Changes in Child

Student's overall behavior compared to last week:

1	2	3	4	5	6	7	8	9	10
Not as good				*Same*					*Better*

Student's concerning behavior	Compared to last time (circle one)	Additional Note
	Not as good Same Better	
	Not as good Same Better	
	Not as good Same Better	
	Not as good Same Better	
	Not as good Same Better	

Student's mood/attitude towards life/school, compared to last week:

1	2	3	4	5	6	7	8	9	10
Not as good				*Same*					*Better*

My experience teaching my student compared to last week:

1	2	3	4	5	6	7	8	9	10
Not as good				*Same*					*Better*

Method	How did the student respond?	Would you do anything differently?

□ **It's very important that I speak with you as soon as possible.**

□ **I need to talk with you within a week.**

_____

_____

_____

_____

_____

_____

_____

_____

_____

_____

_____

_____

_____

_____

_____

_____

_____

_____

The Efficacy of Play Therapy and Filial Therapy with Children: Summary of the Meta-Analytic Findings

Sue Bratton, PhD. LPC. RPT-S

Tammy Rhine. PhD. LPC, *NCC*

Dee Ray, PhD, LPC, NCC, RPT-S

Leslie Jones. PhD, lPC, *NCC*

Child therapists are ethically-bound and accountable to their clients to provide treatments that are most effective; however they have received little help from the scientific community to guide their efforts. Historically, the efficacy of psychological interventions for children has been a basis for controversy and debate among mental health professionals. Not until recently has this issue received national.attention, with the U. S. Public Health Service (2000) emphasizing the critical need for early intervention and empirically-validated treatments that are designed specifically to meet children's unique needs.

Play therapy is a developmentally responsive modality uniquely suited for children to help prevent or resolve psychosocial difficulties and achieve optimal growth and development. Developmentally, children lack the cognitive ability to meaningfully communicate their thoughts, feelings, and experiences through the abstract means of verbal language. The concrete objects (toys, art, etc.) and other play-based experiences provided in

play therapy afford children an age-appropriate and emotionally safe means to express their difficult experiences. For these reasons, play therapy is currently practiced by thousands of clinicians to treat their young clients; however the scientific community has been less enamored, criticizing this modality's lack of an adequate research base to support its practice. Proving the effectiveness of play therapy to third party payors, the legal community, mental health professionals, school administrators, parents, and critics of play therapy is necessary for the acceptance of play therapy as a viable intervention from emotional and/or behavioral difficulties that need responsive services.

Meta-analytic methodology allows the researcher to analyze the effects of a treatment, in this case play therapy, by combining the results of individual studies, thus overcoming the limitations of small sample sizes often found in outcome research in the mental health field. The authors conducted a meta-analysis of 93 controlled outcome studies, published 1953 to

2000, to assess the overall efficacy of play therapy and to determine factors that might impact its effectiveness. The overall mean' treatment effect was 0.80 standard deviations, considered a large treatment effect Further analysis revealed that effects were more positive for humanistic than for non- humanistic treatments, and that utilizing parents in their child's play therapy produced larger overall treatment effects than play therapy conducted by a professional. Play therapy appeared equally effective across age, gender, presenting issue; and clinical vs. psychotherapy, and further suggest that doubts about the efficacy of play therapy can be laid to rest.

Definitions

Play Therapy: a developmentally sensitive therapeutic modality in which a trained play therapist uses the therapeutic powers of play to help clients prevent or resolve psychosocial difficulties and achieve optimal growth and development (Association for Play Therapy,2003)

FilialTherapy: a therapeutic intervention that can help children by teaching parents (and other paraprofessionals such as teachers) basic Child-Centered play therapy principles and methods to use with their children (Guerney, B., Guemey,L.. & Adronico, 1966; Landreth, 1991/2002; Landreth & Bratton, 2006). Parents learn to become a constructive force for change in their children's behaviors and attitudes by utilizing basic play therapy skills in once-a-week 30-minute play sessions with their children. Throughout the process, parents *receive* on-going training and direct supervision from a trained play therapist.

Meta-Analysis: combines the results of individual studies by determining the amount of change of individuals in the treatment group versus those in the control or comparison group and then determining the average amount of change in a set of efficacy studies (Prout & Prout, 1998).Meta-analysis overcomes the limitations of small sample sizes and conflicting findings that may be attributed to small samples and allows broader reaching scientific discovery and more generalized conclusions. An effect size is calculated and reported in a Q score which is essentially the average amount of change in standard deviation units achieved by individuals in a treated group versus the change achieved by members of a control/comparison group for a particular study. An effect size of Q -i· 1.0 represents 'I standard deviation.

Descriptive Data

Total Studies: 93

TotalSubjects: 3263

Mean # of Sessions: 16

Mean Age: 7.0

Gender of Subjects: 2/3 male, 1/3 female

Results

EFFECT SIZE FOR THE TOTAL (93 STUDIES): ES=.80 P<.001

- Effect Size for Play Therapy by Professional (n=67): ES=.72 p<.05
- Effect Size for Play Therapy by Paraprofessionals (n=26): ES=1.05 p<.05
- (Filial therapy studies conducted by parents, teachers, mentors- mostly parents)
- Effect Size for the Parent only Filial Therapy (n=22): ES=1.15 p<.05

Interpretation of Effect Size

According to Cohen (1977), $g = .2$ represents a small effect size; $g = .5$ represents a medium effect size; and $g = .8$ represents a large effect size; therefore, the results of the meta-analysis of play therapy outcome research studies (n=94) reveal a large treatment effect for children receiving play therapy intervention when compared to children receiving no treatment or a non-play therapy intervention.

Implications for Practice and Further Research

- Play therapy is an effective intervention for a broad range of children's problems- across both behavioral and humanistic schools of thought, in various settings, across modalities, across age and gender. However, better designed studies are needed that examine the questions of, is play therapy more or less effective with regard to gender, age, and presenting issue? In addition, an investigation of different theoretical and technical approaches to play therapy and effect on children's outcome related to the above factors would better address the age-old question, which treatment is most effective with which clients, under what circumstances?

- These results strongly point to a greater utilization of Filial Therapy over Play Therapy: Training parents and involving them in their child's play therapy is highly effective, and also has the potential benefit of preventing more severe and costly problems across the lifespan. However, is filial therapy the treatment of choice for all children presenting for play therapy? Studies comparing filial therapy to play therapy by a professional with the same populations are needed to determine if the factors of presenting issue and child's age influence outcome.

- The identified crises in children's mental health services, including the need for more developmentally- responsive interventions that involve the family, provides a sense of urgency for play therapists to utilize these research findings to educate other mental health professionals, third party payors, the legal community, school administrators/teachers and parents to ensure that more children and families receive the help they need.

Note: This information provides a brief summary of the following publication: Bratton, S., Ray, D., Rhine,T., & Jones, L. (2005). The efficacy of play therapy with children: A Meta- analytic review of the outcome research. *Professional Psychology: Research and Practice,* 36(4), 376-390.

For related information, view summary of play therapy and filial therapy research at www.a4pt.org.

* The authors grant permission to duplicate and distribute this 2-page summary for professional use.

Play Therapy Intake Packet

Although it is not necessary to have a comprehensive history, including a biopsychosocial understanding of any child you are using child centered play therapy with, it is helpful. What follows is the complete and comprehensive packet that I use when doing an intake with parents or caregivers prior to engaging the child in her first play therapy session. To be honest, I hardly ever complete the packet in the hour I allot for intake. I have to make decisions about what is most important for my work with each individual child. This changes from case to case and has evolved through my development as a play therapist. Collaboration with other play therapists and clinical supervision have been invaluable in having a solid clinical sense about what is most salient and why. Feel free to copy what would work for you and augment anything as needed. We are in this together.

Integrative Counseling Services, PLLC
Counseling-Consulting-Play Therapy
Jodi Mullen, PhD LMHC NCC RPT-S CCPT-Master - Director
www.integrativecounseling.us

Child Intake

In order for us to be able to fully evaluate your child, please fill out the following information to the best of your ability. We realize that there may be information that you do not remember or have access to, but please do the best that you can. Thank you!

CLIENT IDENTIFICATION

Full Name_____ Nickname_____

Birth date_____ Age_____ Sex: ☐ M ☐ F

School_____ Grade_____

Religion_____ Race_____

Mother's Name_____ Father's Name_____

Address (street) _____ (city) _____ (state) _____ (zip) _____

Home phone #_____ Cell #_____ ☐ Mom ☐ Dad ☐ Other

May we leave a message for you? ☐ Yes ☐ No   Which number? ☐ Cell ☐ Home

Are there custody concerns and if so, is there legal documentation of custody? ☐ Yes ☐ No

REFERRAL SOURCE
Referred by:

☐ Parent/Guardian ☐ Pediatrician ☐ School ☐ EAP ☐ Child Protective Services

☐ Social Services ☐ Court Order ☐ Other_____

Referral's name_____ Title _____

Referral's address (street) _____ (city) _____ (state) _____

(zip)_____ Phone #_____

Do we have your permission to release information to the referring professional when it is appropriate?
☐ Yes ☐ No

PURPOSE OF EVALUATION AT THIS TIME (Please provide a brief summary of the main concerns)

_____

_____

_____

GOALS (What would you like to see counseling do for your child, you, and your family?)_____

_____

_____

OVERALL STRENGTHS (Please describe some of your child's strengths) _____

_____

_____

ACTIVITIES/HOBBIES/SPECIAL INTERESTS _____

_____

_____

PRIOR/CURRENT CONSULTATIONS (Please include contact names and dates with other professionals, therapists, treatment people)

_____

_____

MEDICAL HISTORY

Is your child currently taking any medication? (Please also include frequent use of over the counter medications) ☐ Yes   ☐ No   If yes, list the name of the drug, dosage, and when taken

_____ name of medication

_____ dosage _____ when taken

Please list _current_ medical concerns:

_____

_____

Current pediatrician's name _____ Contact #_____

Other doctors/clinics seen regularly ☐ Yes ☐ No   If yes, describe _____

_____

_____

Please list *past* medical concerns: _____

_____

_____

Any history of head trauma? ☐ Yes ☐ No If yes, describe _____

_____

Prior hospitalizations ☐ Yes ☐No If yes, describe _____

_____

Allergies? ☐ Yes ☐ No   If yes, describe _____

_____

Does your child have any other medical conditions? ☐ Yes ☐ No If yes, describe_____

_____

DEVELOPMENTAL HISTORY:

During pregnancy, did mother:

☐ Drink alcohol   ☐ use drugs   ☐ accident   ☐ illness   ☐ problems with pregnancy

☐ Problems with labor or delivery   If yes, describe _____

_____

Was your child delayed in any of the following areas?

☐ Turning over   ☐ sitting up ☐ crawling ☐ walking alone   ☐ weaning ☐ feeding self

☐ Toilet training ☐ using single words ☐ using sentences ☐ dressing self

☐ Sleeping through the night

Briefly explain any delays: _____

_____

FAMILY HISTORY

What are your family's strengths? _____

_____

_____

What are your family supports? (Church, friends, clubs, etc) _____

_____

Current relationship status: ☐Married ☐Separated ☐Divorced ☐Dating ☐Single

If in a relationship, satisfaction level: ☐ Happy ☐Content ☐Distant ☐Other

Please describe _____

_____

Please list any family history of mental health diagnoses, learning disabilities, trauma, drug and/or alcohol use/abuse, and legal issues: _____

_____

_____

_____

Please list family members and individuals who currently live with the child (please state names, ages, relationship to your child and any problems or strengths in the relationship)

Name	Age	Relationship	Problems/Strengths

Family Stressors (What are the factors that are a source of stress in the family? Check all that apply)

	Current	Past		Current	Past
Parent relationship problems			Legal issues		
Custody/visitation disputes			Parents using alcohol/drugs		
Financial problems			Family illness		
Job loss			Death of a pet		
Housing problems			Other stressors:		

If other stressors please describe: _____

_____

_____

Are there any legal actions that may have impacted your child? Please check all that apply:

	Current	Past		Current	Past
Custody			Visitation		
Adoption			Child Protective Services		
Probation			Other		

Please provide additional information if necessary: _____

_____

Trauma History (Has your child experienced any of the following? Please check all that apply)

	Current	Past		Current	Past
Physical Abuse			Emotional Neglect		
Sexual Abuse			Physical Neglect		
Verbal Abuse			Witness to Domestic Violence		
Person in household who went to prison/jail			Person in household who uses drugs or is a problem drinker		
Parents separated/divorced			Person in household with a mental illness or suicide attempt		
Significant death losses					

If yes, please describe (disclosure, details, any legal action, CPS involvement, police involvement):

_____

_____

Check all areas that apply to your child:

Behavior	Current	Past	Behavior	Current	Past
Crying, sadness, depression			Is overly concerned about things		
Withdrawn			Unusual fears or phobias		
Worries more than other children			Repeats unnecessary act over and over again		
Anxious/nervous			Strange or unusual behaviors		
Panic Attacks			Hallucinations		
Argues a lot			Has rituals/habits/superstitions		
Temper outbursts			Disorientation		

Behavior	Current	Past	Behavior	Current	Past
Easily annoyed by others			Poor appetite		
Irritability/Anger			Over or underweight		
Loss of enjoyment of usual activities			Eats very little/fasts to lose weight		
Expresses a wish to die			Blames others for own mistakes		
Bedtime fears/won't sleep			Does things that annoy others		
Nightmares/night terrors			Swears or uses obscene language		
Tiredness/fatigue			Wanting to run away		
Wakes up very early/unable to go back to sleep			Sneaks out at night		
Restless sleep/wakes frequently			Injures self		
Trouble going to sleep			Vomits intentionally		
Sleeps too much			Soiling (pooping) in pants		
Bedwetting/daytime wetting			Hurts people		
Sleepwalking			Hurts animals		
Low self esteem			Lying/stealing		
Over activity			Destroys property		
Frequently acts w/o thinking			Drug/Alcohol use		
Doesn't finish things			Cigarette use		
Disruptive			Sexual behavior		
Short attention span			Problems with authority		
Daydreams/fantasizes			Problems with the law		
Easily distracted			Twitches or unusual movements		
Low motivation			Disorientation		

What form of discipline do you use in the home? ☐ Time out ☐ Loss of privileges ☐ Grounding
☐ Rewards/incentives ☐ Extra chores ☐ Physical/corporal punishment ☐ Other (describe) _____

_____

_____

RELATIONSHIP/SOCIAL DEVELOPMENT: Check each item that describes your child

	Current	Past		Current	Past
Prefers to be alone			Is oversensitive		
Is alone a lot, but dislikes it and feels lonely			Is picked on a lot		
Is shy			Bullies others		
Has few friends			Teases a lot		
Has many friends			Fights with other kids		
Plays with "problem kids"			Is demanding and bossy		
Plays with younger kids			Poor relationships with peers		
Plays with older kids			Conflict w/parents/step-parents		
Poor relationships with teachers			Has difficulty getting along with brothers and sisters		

SCHOOL: Check any area of concern:

	Current	Past		Current	Past
Dislikes school			Missed many school days		
Works hard but does not do well			Repeated a grade		
Unmotivated/refuses to complete work			Discipline referrals, detentions		
Learning problems			Suspensions (how many? _____)		
Expulsions (how many? _____)					

If your child has been suspended or expelled, please explain: _____

_____

_____

How do teachers describe your child to you? _____

_____

Does your child receive any special services in school? ☐Yes ☐No   If yes, describe _____

_____

BIBLIOGRAPHY

Albon, S. L. (1996). The therapeutic action of play. *Journal of the American Academy of Child and Adolescent Psychiatry, 35*(4), 545-548.

Axline, V. M. (1947). *Play therapy.* New York: Ballantine.

Axline, V. M. (1969). *Play therapy* (Rev. ed.). New York, NY: Ballantine.

Bratton, S. C., Ceballos, P. L., Sheely-Moore, A. I., Meany-Walen, K., Pronchenko, Y., & Jones, L. D. (2013). Head start early mental health intervention: Effects of child-centered play therapy of disruptive behaviors. *International Journal of Play Therapy, 22*(1), 28 – 42.

Burke Harris, N. (2018). *The deepest well: healing the long-term effects of childhood adversity.* Boston, MA: Houghton Mifflin Harcourt.

Clark, A. J. (2010). Empathy and sympathy: Therapeutic distinctions in counseling. *Journal of Mental Health Counseling, 32*(2), 95-101.

Cochran, J.L., & Cochran, N.H. (2017). Effects of child-centered play therapy for students with highly-disruptive behavior in high-poverty schools, *International Journal of Play Therapy, 26*(2), 59–72.

Cochran, J. L., & Cochran, N. H. (2015). *The heart of counseling: Counseling skills through therapeutic relationships* (2nd ed.). New York, NY: Routledge.

Cochran, N. H., Nordling, W. J., & Cochran, J. L. (2010). *Child centered play therapy.* Hoboken, NJ: Wiley.

Crenshaw, D. A., & Kenney-Nozsika, S. (2014). Therapeutic presence in play therapy. *International Journal of Play Therapy, 23*(1), 31–43.

Crenshaw, D. A., & Stewart, A. (Eds.). (2015). *Play therapy: A comprehensive guide to theory and practice.* New York, NY: Guilford Press.

Erdman, P. & Lampe, R. (1996). Adapting basic skills to counsel children. *Journal of Counseling & Development, 74,* 374-377.

Fiorini, J., & Mullen, J. (2006). *Counseling children and adolescents through grief and loss.* Champaign, IL: Research Press.

Gil, E. (2017). *Posttraumatic play in children: What clinicians need to know.* New York, NY: Guilford Press.

Gil, E., & Drewes, A. A. (2005). *Cultural issues in play therapy.* New York, NY: Guilford.

Ginott, H. G. (1961). *Group psychotherapy with children.* New York: McGraw-Hill.

Kestly: T. A. (2014). *The interpersonal neurobiology of play: Brain-building interventions for emotional well-being.* New York, NY: W W Norton& Co.

Killough McGuire, D., & McGuire, D. E. (2001). *Linking parents to play therapy: A practical guide with applications, interventions, and case studies.* Philadelphia: Brunner-Routledge.

Kottman, T. (2010). *Play therapy: Basic and beyond.* Alexandria, VA: American Counseling Association.

Kottman, T. (1999). Play therapy. In A. Vernon (Ed.), *Counseling children and adolescents* (2nd ed.). (pp. 98 -119). Denver, CO: Love Publishing.

Kottman, T. (2001). *Play Therapy: Basic and beyond.* Alexandria, VA: American Counseling Association.

Kottman, T. (2003). *Partners in play: An Adlerian approach to play therapy (2nd ed.).* Alexandria, VA: American Counseling Association.

Kranz, P. L, & Lund, N. L. (1993). Axline's eight principles of play therapy revisited. *International Journal of Play Therapy, 2*(2), 53-60.

Landreth, G. L. (2002). *Play therapy: The art of the relationship (2nd ed.).* New York: Brunner-Routledge.

Landreth, G. L., & Wright, C. S. (1997). Limit setting practices of play therapists in training and experienced play therapists. *International Journal of Play Therapy, 6*(1), 41-62.

Lin, Y., & Bratton, S. (2015). A meta-analytic review of child-centered play therapy approaches. *Journal of Counseling & Development, 93*(1), 45–58.

Moustakas, C. E. (1953*). Children in play therapy: A key to understanding normal and disturbed emotions.* New York, NY: McGraw-Hill.

Mullen, J. A., (2018). Book Review: Doing play therapy: From building the relationship to facilitating change. *American Journal of Play, Fall,* 133-4.

Mullen, J. A. (2018). *Raising freakishly well behaved kids: 20 principles for being the parent your child needs.* LaVergne, TN; Ingram Spark.

Mullen, J. A. (2015). Play therapy supervision. In O'Connor, K.J., Schaefer, C.E., & Braverman, L.D. (Eds.), *Handbook of Play Therapy* (2nd ed). pp.549-560, Wiley.

Mullen, J. A., & Rickli, J. M. (2014). *Child-centered play therapy workbook: A self-directed guide for professionals.* Champaign, IL: Research Press.

Mullen, J. A., & Storie, M. (2011). Treating complicated grief. In Brock, S. & Jimerson, S. (Eds.), *Best Practices in Crisis Prevention and Intervention in the Schools* (2nd ed.). pp.671-679, National Association for School Psychologists.

Mullen, J. A., & Uninsky, P. (2007). *Child-centered play therapy fidelity checklist.* Hamilton, NY: Youth Policy Institute.

Nordling, W. J., & Guerney, L. (1999). Typical stages in the child-centered play therapy process. *The Journal for the Professional Counselor, 14*(1), 17-23.

O'Connor, K. J., Schaefer, C. E., & Braverman, L. D. (2016). *Handbook of play therapy;* (2nd ed). Hoboken, NJ: John Wiley & Sons Inc.

O'Connor, K. J. (2000). *The play therapy primer.* (2nd ed.) New York: John Wiley & Sons.

Orton, G. L. (1996). Strategies for counseling with children and their parents. Pacific Grove, CA: Brooks/Cole.

Pedersen. P. B., & Ivey. A. (1993). *Culture-Centered Counseling and Interviewing Skills.* Connecticut: Praeger.

Phillips, E., & Mullen, J. A. (1999). Client-centered play therapy techniques for elementary school counselors: Building the supportive relationship. *The Journal for the Professional Counselor, 14,* 25-36.

Post, P.B., Phipps, C.B., Camp, A.C., & Grybush, A. L. (2019). Effectiveness of child-centered play therapy among marginalized children. *International Journal of Play Therapy, 28*(2), 88–97.

Ray, D. C. (2016). *Extraordinarily normal: The therapist's guide to child development.* New York, NY: Routledge.

Ray, D. (2004). Supervision of basic advanced skills in play therapy. *Journal of Professional Counseling: Practice, Theory, and Research, 32*(2), 28-41.

Ray, D. (2011). *Advanced play therapy: Essential conditions, knowledge, and skills for child practice*. Milton Park, Oxfordshire, England: Taylor and Francis.

Ray, D., Armstrong, S., Balkin, R., & Jayne, K. (2015). Child centered play therapy in the schools: Review and meta-analysis. *Psychology in the Schools, 52*, 107-123.

Ritzi, R. M., Ray, D. C., Schumann, B. R. (2017). Intensive short-term child-centered play therapy and externalizing behaviors in children. *International Journal of Play Therapy, 26*(1), 33–46.

Rogers, C. (1951). *Client-centered therapy*. Boston: Houghton Mifflin.

Shen, Y. (2017). Play therapy with adolescents in school: Counselor's firsthand experiences. *International Journal of Play Therapy, 26* (2), 84–95.

Stern, M. & Newland, L. M. (1994). Working with children: Providing a framework for the roles of counseling psychologists. *The Counseling Psychologist, 22(3)*, 402-425.

Stulmaker, H. L., & Ray, D. C. (2015). Child-centered play therapy with young children who are anxious: A controlled trial. *Children and Youth Services Review 57*, 127–133.

Tanner, Z., & Mathis, R. D. (1995). A Child-centered typology for training novice play therapists, *International Journal of Play Therapy, 4*(2), 1-13.

Thompson, C. L., & Rudolph, L. B. (2000). *Counseling children*. (5th ed.). Stamford, CT:Brooks/Cole.

VanFleet, R., Sywulak, A. E., & Caparosa, C. (2010). *Child-centered play therapy*. New York, NY: Guilford.

Van der Kolk, B. A. (2014). *The body keeps the score: mind, brain, and body in the transformation of trauma*. New York, NY & London: Allen Lane, Penguin Books.

Vargas, L. A., & Koss-Choino, J. D. (1992). *Working with culture: Psychotherapeutic interventions with ethnic minority children and adolescents*. San Francisco, CA: Jossey-Bass.

Wheeler, N., & Dillman Taylor, D. (2016). Integrating interpersonal neurobiology with Play Therapy. *International Journal of Play Therapy, 25*(1), 24–34.

APPENDIX A

Answers and Explanations

Feeling Words: Sample Answers

1. Annoyed That <u>bothers</u> or <u>bugs</u> you. Dominant US culture: Sigh or eye roll

2. Ashamed You felt <u>embarrassed</u>.

3. Bored Yawn. You are <u>tired</u> of this.

4. Brave You feel like a <u>superhero</u>. You're <u>not scared</u>.

5. Cooperative You are <u>working</u> as part of a team. You are <u>working</u> together with me.

6. Curious You are <u>wondering</u>. You're <u>unsure</u>.

7. Defective You feel <u>broken</u>, like there's <u>something wrong</u> with you.

8. Disappointed That's <u>upsetting</u>. "Ugh." You are feeling <u>sad</u> mixed with <u>mad</u>.

9. Disconnected It's like <u>no one cares</u>. You feel <u>lonely</u>. You feel all <u>alone</u>.

10. Enthusiastic "Wow!" You are <u>excited</u>. "Yippee!"

11. Frustrated "Grrr!" You are really <u>annoyed</u>, <u>fed up</u>, <u>mad</u>.

12. Hopeless You feel like <u>giving up</u>. You think <u>why bother?</u>

13. Insecure You're <u>unsure</u> of yourself. You don't feel like you <u>can</u>.

14. Malicious You feel <u>mean and sneaky</u>. You want others to <u>hurt</u>.

15. Obstinate Dominant US culture: fold arms over chest, stamp feet. You are <u>not going to</u> move, stop, or change. You're feeling <u>stubborn</u>.

16. Overwhelmed This is too much for you. "Sigh." Dominant US culture: put head down and shake "no."

17. Satisfied You're <u>all set</u>, <u>proud</u>. "Whoa."

18. Tentative You're <u>unsure</u>. You want to <u>take your time</u>.

19. Unpopular You feel like <u>no one likes you</u>. You're feeling <u>left out</u>.

20. Vulnerable It's all <u>scary</u>. You're <u>not sure</u> you can <u>trust</u>. You don't feel <u>safe</u>.

Reflecting feeling: Let's practice: Sample Answers

Possible feelings:

Curious

Delighted

Pleased

Determined

In charge

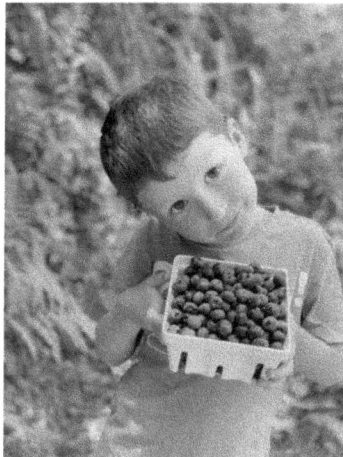

Possible feelings:

Curious

Thoughtful

Sweet

Generous

Possible feelings:

Silly

Happy

Awkward

Unsure

Confused

Possible feelings:

Fresh

Silly

Annoyed

Sassy

Powerful

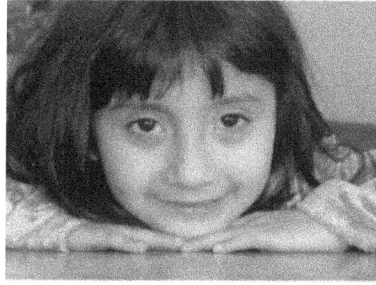

Possible feelings:

Content

Pleased

Delighted

Dreamy

Relaxed

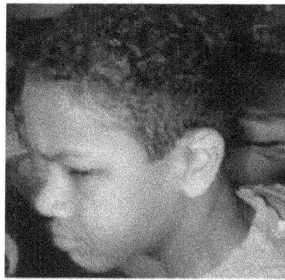

Possible feelings:

Angry

Mad

Upset

Hurt

Troubled

Reflection of feeling: Exercise Sample Answers

1. You were very scared. _X_ → You were afraid.

2. You want that toy. ___ → You are determined.

3. That was surprising. _X_ → That was unexpected.

4. You are so tired. _X_ → You feel sleepy.

5. You are sad. _X_ → You feel unhappy.

6. That was a good one. ___ → You feel good about that.

7. That shocked you. _X_ → That was unbelievable.

8. You feel like a superhero. ___ → You are feeling brave.

9. You are angry. _X_ → You are super mad.

10. That was frustrating. _X_ → You got fed up.

Empathizing versus Giving Solutions: Sample Answers

1. Don't cry. <u>You are feeling sad about ...</u>

2. Don't worry. <u>Some things really worry you.</u>

3. It will be okay. <u>You are scared things won't be okay.</u>

4. It's not a big deal. <u>It's a big deal to you.</u>

5. You can't win them all. <u>It's hard for you when you don't win.</u>

6. That's life. <u>You feel that was unfair.</u>

7. It could be worse. <u>It's really bad for you.</u>

8. You'll do fine. <u>You're worried you won't do well.</u>

9. Everything will be all right. <u>You're not sure things will work out.</u>

10. It's not that important. <u>It's important to you.</u>

11. You'll get another chance. <u>You are afraid you're not going to get another chance.</u>

12. Some problems solve themselves. <u>This is a serious problem to you.</u>

13. There's always a bright side. <u>You're not sure things will ever be better.</u>

14. People grow from experiences like this. <u>This has been very hard for you.</u>

15. It's for your own good. <u>You don't like what's happening.</u>

Tracking: Exercise Sample Answers

1. Child stands on the chair. <u>You are making yourself bigger.</u>

2. Child jumps up and down. <u>You are showing me how you can jump.</u>

3. Child uses toy food to "feed" the baby doll. <u>You're feeding that one.</u>

4. Child tried several crayons. <u>You wanted to see if those work.</u>

5. Child looks out the window after hearing a sudden noise. <u>You are going to see what that was all about.</u>

Should you set the limit? Sample Answers

Here I will try to explain why I would or would not set the limit. I will also offer an example of a limit with the redirection. The redirection lets children know what they can do and the limit emphasizes what they cannot do. There are many alternative redirections, and my goal here is to give you an idea. You will notice that for most examples, I have given you an example of how I would set the limit if indeed a limit needed to be set. You will also see that for many of the circumstances listed below, there is not a clear cut answer.

• Child wants to leave session early—no

There is no reason to keep a child in the playroom if she wants to leave. It is important to recognize that keeping a child in the room will strain your relationship and is not therapeutic. Would you try and force an adult to stay in a therapy session if she wanted to leave? Probably not. Children rarely want to leave the playroom early, but when they do, honor their wish. This can be made less complicated by notifying caregivers and other stakeholders that children will sometimes need to leave early for therapeutic and safety reasons. Therefore, if a child needs to leave or if they "limit out", someone will be there waiting and will not be surprised if they do not stay the full time (30 minutes).

Limit: Make sure you let the child know that if she decides to leave, the session is over. "Paulette, you can leave now if you like, but that means we are not coming back into this special room today"

• Child wants to stand on the chair—yes/no

This one is a judgment call. If you feel like the child can be safe, I do not see a reason to set the limit.

I make sure to stay close by in case the child gets wobbly and needs immediate physical support. You will find that children are attracted to standing on chairs and other structures. I think one reason for this is that typically they are not allowed to play in such a way and secondly, kids like to make themselves bigger. The perspective from their culture is that power and control are connected to how big you are.

Limit: "Yuka, you cannot stand on the chair because it is unsafe, but you can raise your arms up high over your head, if you want to be big."

• Child spanks you—yes

There is no reason to let a child hit or hurt you, but many children will attempt this behavior because that's the way they are/were treated. Always limit this behavior.

Limit: "Shoshana, you cannot hit or hurt me in here. You wanted me to feel what that's like. You can pretend to hit me or hit the doll instead."

• Child writes on face with marker—yes/no

I won't let children write on my face with marker. I am not comfortable with having that done to my face. Never let a child do something to you in the playroom that makes you feel uncomfortable. When you feel uncomfortable, you are not able to adhere to the Eight Basic Principles.

I will let children write on their own faces if they are not going back to class or somewhere other than home after their appointment. It would be distracting and potentially embarrassing, as even the washable marker does not come off all the way.

Limit: "Alexandros, I see you want to decorate your face. You are feeling silly. One thing you cannot do in here is write on your face with markers. You can write on the paper or on the bop bag."

• Child yells swear words, yes/no

This depends on the setting. If I am in a setting where this would not be an issue for confidentiality, or disturbance to others, then I would not set the limit.

Limit: "Rory, you cannot yell those words in here. You can say them but not yell them. People walking by might get scared by those words."

• Child wants to take clothes off—yes

I will let children take off their shoes and socks. For some children this is how they get comfortable or demonstrate their comfort. I have had children in the playroom ask (and not ask) to take their clothes off. This makes the playroom a potentially unsafe place. I would never allow it.

Limit: "Japhy, you are very hot in here today, but one thing you cannot do is take your shirt off. You can take your sneakers off if you want to."

• Child plays with your hair—yes/no

I guess I don't think you should really allow this because of hygiene reasons, but I include this example to talk to you about another reason to set limits. I always set this limit with children, not because a child playing with my hair makes me uncomfortable, but quite to the contrary, I really like it. The playroom is not a place for me to get my needs met.

Limit: "Chloe, remember I told you there are some things you cannot do in here. One thing you cannot do is play with my hair. You wanted to show me you care about me. You can play with the doll's hair."

• Child kisses you—yes

As I have said before, the children you do play therapy with will love and adore you. I want to set good boundaries and not confuse them about the nature of our relationship so I set the limit. It is, however, important to view this and the spectrum of behaviors displayed through a cultural lens. Please account for the culture of childhood, as well as other salient cultural identifications with each individual child.

Limit: "Young, remember I told you there are some things you cannot do in here. One thing you cannot do is kiss me on the face. I know you like me so much. You can blow me a kiss instead."

• Child wants to tie you up—yes/no

Here again, this has to do with your comfort level. I let kids tie me up because it does not bother me and I have never felt like I will not be able to react or get out.

Limit: "Gerry, remember there are some things you cannot do in here. You cannot tie me up. You can put the jump rope on me and I will pretend I am tied up. You wanted me to feel trapped."

• Child brings in toys from home—no

I do not limit this. I think children bringing toys from home is like a gift. It is a way of sharing their bigger world with me. If the toy is dangerous, then I would set a limit.

Limit: "Dakota, you are so proud of your new pocket knife, but that would make the playroom an unsafe place. You can have your Dad hold it until our time is up."

xChild wants to take home artworkyes/no

I will let children bring home paintings and drawings they have made, but not clay creations. I would

never have any clay if I allowed this. I will not let children take home creations that have swear or hate language written on them. Those words are allowed in the playroom only.

Limit: "Jeff, you really want to take that picture home with you. That picture has to stay here because the words you wrote on it are only allowed in the special playroom. You can make a picture without those words and take that home."

• Child sucks on baby bottle—no

Remember, regression is a typical play style in the therapeutic playroom. Make sure you keep the bottles sanitized. I see no reason to limit this behavior and, in fact, too often children are ridiculed for acting younger than they actually are.

Limit: "Ginny, you are really curious about that bottle. One thing you cannot do is put it in your mouth because I forgot to clean it. I will clean it now if you want, so you can use it the way you want to."

• Child shoots at you with toy gun—yes

Even suction cup or foam darts can hurt. I do not let children shoot me or themselves in the playroom.

Limit: "Marta, remember I told you there are some things you cannot do in here. One thing you cannot do is shoot me with the dart gun. I know you are so mad at me. You can shoot at the walls, or bop bag or dolls."

• Child says nasty things to you—no

It is so important that children be able to say what they need to say in the playroom, regardless of how rude it is. Remember, children often use harsh language because this language is what they are used to hearing. Children also want to make sure you understand their perspective, so many of them will treat you how they feel they are treated.

Non-limit: "Sophie, you want me to know what it's like to be called names."

• Child exposes his/her private parts—yes

This may seem like a "no-brainer" so I want to make it very clear. There is no reason a child should be allowed to expose him or herself in session. This will happen because all of you will work with sexually abused children (whether you know it or not). Children who have been sexually abused are likely to have precarious boundaries. Some will show you their private parts because that is how other adults have engaged them. Rather then deal with the anticipatory anxiety of their safety, they expose themselves to you as a subconscious test, "Can I trust this one (adult)?" When you set this limit, make sure you identify what private part you are talking about because many children who have been sexually victimized are not aware that parts of their bodies are private because their private parts were made public.

Limit: "Teddy, there are some things you cannot do in here. You cannot pull down your pants and show me your penis. Your penis is a private part of your body. You were not sure if you could trust me not to hurt you. You can pull down the doll's pants."

NO Questions: Exercise Sample Answers

Exercise 1

1. Why did you do that? <u>Sometimes you do things so fast you do not think about the consequences.</u>
2. What could you have done differently? <u>You came up with a solution.</u>
3. How would you like to change this? <u>This is not for you, and you wish there was another way.</u>
4. Why do you think that happened? <u>You are confused about why that happened.</u>
5. Do you want me to color with you? <u>I cannot tell if you want me to color with you.</u>

Exercise 2

1. What time is it? <u>You are concerned about the time.</u>
2. Do other kids come here? <u>Sometimes you wonder if I only play with you.</u>
3. Do you have kids? <u>You are curious about me.</u>
4. What's this toy called? <u>You feel unsure.</u>
5. Why do you talk like that? <u>It's annoying you.</u>
6. Can I swear in here? <u>You aren't sure you can trust what I said about saying anything.</u>
7. Can I stay more minutes? <u>You feel rushed, like you need more time.</u>
8. Why can't I spank you? <u>You are confused why I won't let you hurt me.</u>
9. Do you love me? <u>You are worried that I do not care about you.</u>
10. Can I leave now? <u>You are feeling ready to go.</u>

Exercise 3

1. Are you a boy or a girl? <u>You are unsure about me.</u>
2. How come you're so fat? <u>You're surprised.</u>
3. Would you like to see my penis? <u>Set the limit then reflect this one. Fred, in this room you do not show your private parts. That would be unsafe. Your</u>

penis is private. You wanted to feel in charge.

4. You're breath smells, what did you eat for lunch? <u>You notice lots of things.</u>

5. Do you want to smell my fart? <u>You want to know that I accept you no matter what.</u>

NO Praise: Exercise Sample Answers

1. Greg: "I did it. Do you like it?"

Praiser: "I am so proud of you, it's awesome."

Play therapist: <u>You are proud you did it and are curious what I think.</u>

2. Jaielle: : "Here catch."

Praiser: "That was a good throw."

Play Therapist: <u>You made it come right to me.</u>

3. Tiki: "Look how tall I made the building."

Praiser: "Wow, you did a great job."

Play therapist: <u>You are surprised with what you are able to do.</u>

4. Juanita: (Puts on princess crown). "I am the fairest in the land."

Praiser: "You look beautiful."

Play therapist: <u>You are feeling so pretty and special.</u>

5. Griffin: Draws a picture, looks at you and smiles.

Praiser: "That's a terrific picture."

Play Therapist: <u>You are proud of what you created.</u>

What about...: Sample Answers

1. What if the child will not talk?

If a child chooses not to verbally communicate in Child-Centered Play Therapy it is not a big deal. The play therapist is alert to respond to the child's facial expressions, body language, vocalizations and play. Remember to watch the child's facial expressions and not only what he is playing with.

2. What if the child wants to bring in a friend, parent, sibling?

I am reluctant to allow a child to bring a friend into the therapeutic playroom unless I have permission from that child's (the friend) parent. In clinical settings I will allow parents and siblings to join the last five minutes unless the intervention is best suited to be sibling play therapy or a child- parent play therapy.

3. What about sand, paint, water, MESSES?

The play therapist should not include any of the above materials in her playroom if she cannot tolerate the potential mess. Children need to make messes in play therapy to demonstrate chaos or as a metaphor for life's messes. Make sure to schedule ample time between sessions for cleaning up (playroom messes are taken care of by the play therapist). For an alternative and collaborative clean up see Terry Kottman, (2003). *Partners in play. An Adlerian approach to play therapy (2nd ed.).*

4. What do you do when the child won't leave the playroom?

See page 33 for closing a session.

5. What about swearing, cussing, hate language?

In the playroom, children need to be able to say anything. Some children think "bad words" are words like drunk, penis, hate. Typically, children do not use disturbing language, but there are some who are experts. These words have power and children know that. When they use "bad language" it is helpful to view them through a lens of power. Do not use these words in your responses to them.

6. What about having toy guns in the playroom?

Some settings, like schools, may not permit toy guns in the playroom. Some parents do not want their child to play with guns. It's good policy to alert parents that there are toy guns and other weapons in the playroom. Children will find a way to demonstrate aggression even without a toy gun so it's not necessary, only recommended. Additionally, I've had some children use the toy gun as a "nail gun" for construction play and as a fishing pole for competency play.

7. What if kids want to leave the session early?

In clinical settings it's best to advise the person who has transported the child to session not to leave the premises so that if the child limits out early or chooses to leave the session early, she can. There is no reason to force a child to stay in session, as you wouldn't do that to an adult. This may be a way the child can test the therapist or take control. Very infrequently a child will want to leave early. The child's wish should be honored and respected.

8. What about settings where noise in the playroom is a factor to others in close proximity?

Oftentimes playrooms are located close to administrative offices or classrooms. Disturbing noises can make adults and children outside of the playroom uncomfortable and put the play therapist and children in a precarious situation where play therapist, play therapy and child are evaluated unfavorably. It is helpful not to limit what children say, but how loudly they say it. I will let children pretend to yell or make loud noises but not at a level that would disturb others. This creates social awareness and empathy.

9. What if a child is being rude to the play therapist?

In the playroom children often treat the play therapist how they are treated, and sometimes that means children will be rude and disrespectful to the play therapist. It is important to respond to the behavior and not the child. In many cases children are testing the play therapist "if I am nasty with you will you still care about me?"

10. What if the child tells others she can use bad words in session?

Children are usually amazed that they can say anything in the playroom. There are some children who will take you up on the offer to "say anything". However, my experience with children is that most children do not take advantage of this privilege, yet they do recognize it's a privilege so they brag about the playroom.

11. What about children putting toys in their mouths?

Take care in evaluating if toys can be choking hazards and do not include them in the room. It is important to keep toys clean and disinfected. Make determinations based on safety and hygiene.

12. What about children breaking toys?

Toys will break and children will have varying reactions including fear, denial, even pleasure. It's important to reflect the feeling of the child. It is also important to be thoughtful about toys and not put expensive toys or toys you feel a sentimental attachment to in the playroom. Broken toys should be removed from the playroom because they can be dangerous and, furthermore, broken toys send a message to children that they are not important.

13. What if they want to bring in a toy from home?

I think it is a "gift" when children bring a toy from home. My perspective is that the child is sharing part of home with me, and showing me what is important to him. Even when children have brought hand-held video games, it has proven to be an opportunity to gain a deeper understanding of the child's phenomenological world.

14. What about interruptions from others during play therapy sessions?

When the play therapy session gets interrupted, I believe I owe the child that time. If there is a fire drill and 12 minutes are taken up I will say to the child, "Next time I need to give you some extra time because we got interrupted." If we are intruded on by an adult, for whatever reason, I will also give the child back the time. "Claire, I'm sorry the principal walked right into our session. I owe you time because that was your time to have my attention."

15. What if a child discloses abuse during a session?

Different settings have different policies about mandated reporting. Follow the protocol of your setting. Additionally, mandated reporters are not investigators. You do not need to determine if the child has been abused, but you do need to assess for safety. It is important to remember your multiple roles here as mandated reporter and clinician. I stick to Child-Centered Play Therapy during the session and move to assessing for imminent safety immediately following the session. I do not want to jeopardize my relationship with the child.

16. What if a child doesn't feel well and does not want to play or participate?

It's the child's choice whether to play or not. Follow the child's lead.

17. How can play therapists honor diversity?

There are many ways play therapists can honor diversity. Selection of toys can be a tangible and observable way that the richness of diversity can be appreciated. Multicultural dolls, dollhouse figures and crayons/markers are easily available. Additionally, food, kitchen tools, and musical toys, are culturally-centric. Play therapists should be have an array of these toys. (See Gil, E. & Drewes, A. A. (2005). *Cultural Issues in Play Therapy.* for additional suggestions.)

18. What do you do when a child tells you they love you?

As a play therapist, you will be a very special person to children. You can expect children will love you and tell you. Although you may care for, even love your child clients, it would at best be confusing for you to self-disclose your feelings to them. Here again, it is best to stick to the process of Child-Centered Play Therapy. Respond to the child through a listening response such as, "you really care for me," or "you feel so connected to me."

19. What should you do if the child-client falls asleep in session?

That child must feel very safe and, of course, very tired. It would not be therapeutic to awaken him. He is getting a basic need met. Let him sleep until the five minute warning.

Evaluating the impact of the Play Therapist's Responses: Sample Answers

The play therapist should be able to assess the ongoing impact of her responses to the child. It is the play therapist's responsibility to ascertain when responses are accurate, inaccurate, therapeutic, non- therapeutic, tolerable, and/or threatening to the child.

Those of you who like things to be clear-cut or distinct are not going to appreciate this…. There are few clear-cut answers with regard to this matrix. However, the reaction you get from children to the responses you make in play therapy sessions should be evaluated regularly. The process of evaluation is complex and oftentimes leads to more questions. It is the attention that you are giving to the child, session, and practice of play therapy that will facilitate your growth into a competent and confident practitioner.

Behavior	Accurate	Inaccurate	Therapeutic	Non-Therapeutic	Tolerable	Threatening
1. Child moves closer to play therapist.	X		X		X	
2. Child moves away from play therapist.	X	X		X		X
3. Play intensifies.	X	X	X	X	X	
4. Child use play therapist's words.	X		X		X	

1. Child moves closer to play therapist.

When the play therapist makes a response that the child views as representing his thoughts or feelings, the child may respond by moving closer in proximity to the play therapist.

2. Child moves away from play therapist.

Conversely, if the child experiences the response of the play therapist as inaccurate, non-therapeutic, or threatening, the child is likely to increase the physical distance between self and play therapist. It's the child's way of saying, "That response didn't work." If the response was accurate in this case the play therapist may have made the response before the child could handle it.

3. Play intensifies.

The child's play can intensify in the playroom for several reasons. It is the play therapist's ability to read the contextual cues to determine why the play intensified. The child's play intensifies when you are accurate because he feels validated and gets excited recognizing that his communication to you was successful. The child's play intensifies when the play therapist is inaccurate as a means of reiterating the communication. It's the child's way of saying it again and louder hoping that you will "get it" this time. The child's play may intensify because the therapist has made a response that feels therapeutic or because the response is viewed as non-therapeutic and the child feels the need to intensify the play as a means of giving you another chance to demonstrate the Child-Centered philosophy. The child experiences what the play therapist says as safe and therefore intensifies her play to now show you the degree of what she is feeling.

4. Child use play therapist's words.

Children will use the words of the play therapist when they feel connected to the play therapist. This happens as a result of reflecting the child's feelings accurately, making responses that help the child heal, grow or change, and are tolerable to the child by not pushing the child to your adult-centric agenda or pace.

5. Child corrects play therapist.   X   X   X

If a child corrects the play therapist it is likely that the response of the play therapist was inaccurate. Feeling safe enough to correct an adult and feeling sure of yourself also means this reaction is likely to happen in a therapeutic moment. Furthermore, a child may correct the play therapist because the play therapist has stripped the child's protective defenses and, therefore, the child views the play therapist's response as threatening. The child corrects the play therapist as a way of recreating the defense.

6. Child turns away from play
   therapist.

Sometimes the play therapist will move too quickly or deeply in his or her reflections of feeling. This can be unsettling for children. Both accurate and inaccurate responses may be met with the child turning away from the therapist. This is more typical of inaccurate responses, but would also be indicative of accurate responses that can be characterized by too deep, too soon. Likewise, a child will turn away from the play therapist if the comment made by the play therapist is viewed as non-therapeutic or threatening.

7. Child invites play therapist
   into play.

Children will include the play therapist in their play if they feel safe, comfortable, listened to and understood.

8. Child tells play therapist to
   shut up, stop talking.

This kind of reaction to the play therapist's responses usually means that the response was off target, non-therapeutic and scary to the child. It may also be the reaction of a child who cannot tolerate having his feelings reflected back to him. I had this happen regularly with a child I worked with who was bent on not feeling. When I continued to reflect her feelings, even saying "You hate feeling", she taped my mouth shut.

9. Child nods "yes" after   X   X   X   X
   response.

This is another behavior where sub-culture and context play a huge role in the accurate assessment of the interplay between the play therapist's response and the child's response. The child may agree because he feels validated, or because the child thinks he should not acknowledge that you are wrong, or because what you just said felt therapeutic, or because what you said seemed insensitive, but the child believes he is supposed to agree and abdicate to his elders. The child could say yes because that's how he responds when an adult says anything to him and he is scared to say no or because you demonstrated to him that you accept him as he is. As you can see, these behaviors and what they may mean in the playroom are embedded in context.

10. Child wants to end session.   X   X   X   X

This can be a behavioral response to an accurate response on the part of the play therapist or it can be a way for the child to communicate that the play therapist went too deep, too soon. It also may be the child's way of demonstrating that she does not feel understood, respected, accepted or even safe.

11. Child's play changes   X   X   X   X   X   X
    abruptly.

The child's play is typically additive if you are accurate, therapeutic and/or making tolerable responses. Just because the child's play changes abruptly does not mean the opposite assessment should be made. Children's play can change abruptly for any of the following reasons (this is not an exhaustive list): the child becomes distracted by another toy, the child feels pressured to play with a particular toy, the child feels validated, the child feels misunderstood, the child feels safe to try something new, the child feels threatened and tries to achieve a sense of safety and security by changing play.

12. Child's play is additive.   X   X   X

Children's play is communication; therefore, adding to their play is adding to their story. Children won't "tell" you more if you are not making accurate, therapeutic and tolerable responses.

13. Child smiles.   X   X   X   X   X   X

This is another behavior where sub-culture and context play a huge role in the accurate assessment of the interplay between the play therapist's response and the child's response. The child may smile because she feels validated, or because she thinks it's funny that you are wrong, or because what you just said felt therapeutic, or because what you said seemed stupid and had no therapeutic value. The child could smile because that's how she responds when an adult says anything to her or because you demonstrated to her that you accept her as she is. These behaviors and what they may mean in the playroom are embedded in context.

15. Child ignores the play   X   X   X   X
    therapist.

Sometimes the child will ignore you because (this should sound familiar) the play therapist made a response that scared the child because it went too deep, too soon. However, for the most part this kind of behavioral reaction by a child to the play therapist would suggest that the play therapist did not communicate accurate empathic understanding, unconditional positive regard or acceptance. The child is left feeling disconnected, unheard and unsafe.

APPENDIX B

Training and Continuing Education Opportunities

Integrative Counseling Services offers a variety of workshops, trainings, and self-study courses taught by licensed mental health counselors, graduate-level college professors, and certified play therapists. **We are an approved provider for Continuing Education credits (CEs) for Licensed Mental Health Counselors (LMHCs), Licensed Clinical Social Workers (LCSWs), and Registered Play Therapists (RPTs) and want to help you earn your credits through our education services!** We also offer CEs for **National Certified Counselors (NCCs) but currently only for our LIVE, IN-PERSON Training.**

Live, In-Person Training

We also offer live trainings and in-person trainings, which enable you to earn contact continuing education credits. These live events are incredibly helpful if you are a hands-on learner and learn by doing! Many of the trainings involve practicing the theory and technique with others at your evel. Our participants leave feeling confident and ready to bring these approaches into their clinical work!

Some of the topics we cover in our live trainings include:

- Sand Tray Play Therapy
- Child-Centered Play Therapy Basic Training
- How Play Therapists Can Engage Parents and Professionals
- Playful Supervision for Play Therapists
- Home-Based Play Therapy
- Play Therapy with Sexually Traumatized Children

To see our schedule, visit our main website: www.integrativecounseling.us

Self-Study Online Training

If you enjoy learning in the convenience of your home and at your pace, we offer a variety of self-study courses. These courses enable you to earn non-contact continuing education credits and build your knowledge and expertise entirely on your own. The courses feature recorded lectures and recorded trainings with our qualified instructors and clinicians, and we include various links to other outside resources you might find helpful!

To learn more about these self-study courses, or to start earning your non-contact CEs today, visit:

www.integrativecounseling.us/self-study

Some of the topics currently available are:

- *Play Therapy Basic Training (2 CEs)*
- *Adolescent Play Therapy (3 CEs)*
- *How Play Therapists Can Engage Parents and Professionals (3 CEs)*
- *History and Foundations of Play Therapy (2 CEs)*
- *Gestalt Play Therapy: The Violet Oaklander Approach (2 CEs)*
- *Supervision Can Be Playful (1 CE)*
- *Play Therapy with Sexually Traumatized Children (4 CEs)*

Continuing Education

The Association for Play therapy allows 18-36 continuing education hours required for registration renewal to be earned through non-contact hours. In order to assist your efforts to earn play therapy continuing educations hours, you are invited to:

1. Carefully read the discussions included in this workbook.
2. Use the exercises in this workbook to reinforce and solidify skills.
3. Correctly answer all the questions on the following pages.
4. Copy (or tear out) and mail this form and the following pages to Integrative Counseling Services, PLLC
5. Enclose a $10 *non-refundable* processing fee.

ICS will score your responses and, if all are correct, you will receive a certificate for 2 clock hours (non- contact) of APT approved continuing education. No partial credit will be given.

Name:_____

Address:

Street:

City:

State:

Zip:

Phone:

Email:

Signature:

Date:

Please mail or fax to:

Continuing Education Director

Integrative Counseling Services, PLLC

5 West Cayuga Street

Oswego, NY 13126

Fax: 1-866-323-6619

Non-Contact Continuing Education Credits:

Integrative Counseling Services, PLLC is approved by The Association for Play Therapy to offer continuing education specific to play therapy. Our provider number is 06-168. Integrative Counseling Services, PLLC maintains responsibility for the program.

Quiz for Non-Contact Continuing Education Credits

Direction: Select one answer for each question by circling the letter of the best answer.

1. It is okay for the play therapist to make mistakes in the session because

   a. Children usually don't care what you say in the session

   b. Children can correct you and it can be empowering c.

   Children often don't realize your mistake

   d. You can correct it later

2. The reason asking questions is not appropriate in Child-Centered Play Therapy,

   a. Once you ask a question, you are leading

   b. Questions tend to rush the process

   c. Children sometimes don't know the answer

   d. All of the above

3. When you clarify something in role-play, it is okay to use _____ technique.

   a. Talking by writing

   b. Being student

   c. Whisper

   d. Pretending

4. When the child invites and directs you in role-play, your priority is

   a. Reflection

   b. Tracking

   c. Follow their lead and stay in the role

   d. Confrontation

5. The reason taggers should be avoided is

    a. It sounds like you are unsure about what you said

    b. It is a sign of dominance

    c. It sounds friendly

    d. Both a & b are correct

6. When children ask about a toy first time, the best response is

    a. "They're blocks."

    b. "What do you think?"

    c. "You're not sure what it is."

    d. "You know what it is."

7. Toys in the playroom should allow children to experience everything below **except**

    a. Expression

    b. Regression

    c. Aggression

    d. Digression

8. One of the skills which shows the play therapist's attentiveness and acceptance is

    a. Tracking

    b. Praising

    c. Whispering

    d. Questioning

9. When the child says "Did you watch? I made it!!", the appropriate response is

    a. "Wow, you are good."

    b. "I'm proud of you."

    c. "You are proud and very excited."

    d. "You are the best I've ever seen."

10. The following are all examples of "firsts" **except**

   a. The child made eye contact

   b. The child invited the therapist into his/her play

   c. The child wrote his name on paper, just like the previous session

   d. The child said "thank you"

11. Setting limits is important because children need

   a. help to define their boundaries

   b. to feel safe

   c. to be able to explore their environment

   d. all of the above

12. When you set limits,

   a. You should set as many limits as you can

   b. You shouldn't set more than five limits in one session

   c. You should know your personal limits

   d. You need to make a note and put it on the wall so that the child can remember

13. When children don't talk in the session,

   a. Ask about his favorite color and start a social conversation

   b. Respond to the child's non-verbal communication

   c. Pick out some toys the child might be interested in and give them to the child

   d. Leave the child and do your work

14. When the child says she wants to leave the room before the session is over

     a. Let her leave

     b. Explain to her that she doesn't need to do anything, but that she needs to stay whole session in the playroom

     c. Ask the reason

     d. Convince the child that she wants to stay

15. In order to make children easily recognize that the session is coming to a close, the play therapist should

     a. Tell them the time every five minutes

     b. Give them five minute and one minute warnings before the end of session

     c. There is no need to acknowledge the session is almost over, only that it is over

     d. Make a special sign between you and the child, and give the sign to the child five minutes before the end of the session

16. When the child is reluctant to leave the playroom, the play therapist reflects his feelings and

     a. Forces the child to leave the room

     b. Leaves the child alone in the room

     c. Turns off the light and opens the door

     d. Asks the caregiver to remove the child from the room

17. Once you set a limit, and the child breaks the limit again you should

     a. Give the child one more warning to remind the child about the limit

     b. Give the child three more warnings to remind the child about the limit

     c. Repeat the limit until they stop breaking the limit

d. Tell the child that the session will be over if the child breaks the limit again

18. When children use "bad words" in the play room,

    a. You should use those words in order to be connected with the children
    b. Teach them that those words are not appropriate
    c. Let them use those words, but you don't use them
    d. Pretend that you are surprised

19. When the child struggles to open a box, the best response is

    a. "Do you want me to help you?"
    b. "There is a lock in the front."
    c. "You are trying so hard to open it."
    d. "You are the best at trying."

20. You can assess your responses to children by evaluating their behaviors such as

    a. Children move away from (or close to) you
    b. Children begin to use the play therapist's words
    c. Children change their play abruptly
    d. All of the above

21. The Child-Centered Play Therapy approach is considered:

    a. Phenomenological
    b. Humanistic
    c. Neither a or b
    d. Both a and b

22. In play therapy toys are considered

    a. The words

    b. The language

    c. The rule

    d. The reason

23. Toys in the playroom should be

    a. Battery operated

    b. Durable

    c. Easy to replace

    d. Both b & c are correct

24. RPT stands for

    a. Realistic Play Therapy

    b. Registered Play Therapist

    c. Regulated Play Therapy

    d. Rogerian Play Therapist

25. The author argues that all of the following are appropriate for the play therapist to do in Child- Centered Play Therapy **except**:

    a. Self-disclosure

    b. Set limits

    c. Reflection of feeling

    d. Follow the child's lead

Play Therapy Basic Training

LAST WORD: SO WHAT DO YOU BELIEVE?

Remember I said Child-Centered Play Therapy is a philosophy and not a set of techniques. Let's assess how you think, feel and what you believe about children.
Direction: Fill in the blanks.

1. Children are _____.
2. Children like _____.
3. Children want _____.
4. Children believe _____.
5. Children wish _____.
6. Children have _____.
7. Children see _____.
8. Children try _____.
9. Children love _____.
10. Children hate _____.
11. Children need _____.

- A Long Hard Look-

After completing the exercise, take a good look at your answers. Do your answers reflect a Child-Centered philosophy? If not how flexible are your answers? Is the Child-Centered philosophy something you can live by?

ACKNOWLEDGEMENTS

Play therapy has changed my life. It gave me purpose, a way of connecting to children in my professional and personal life, and connected me to the most devoted, creative, and fun mental health practitioners. Most significantly, doing play therapy and being a play therapist, has been an honor and privilege as I have had over 25 years of teachers in the form of children.

I am abundantly grateful for all the children I have been blessed to work with. These children taught me (and still do) about play therapy, childhood, and myself. They taught me to be grateful, what resiliency is all about, and how play and hope are connected. I want to thank the parents and caregivers of the children I have worked with professionally; they trusted me with their children. I took that responsibility seriously and still do.

I am surrounded by supportive people. I have a work-family at Integrative Counseling Services who are dedicated to play therapy and children. We share common goals to provide children with quality, respectful mental health services. I am especially grateful to the "Creativity Club," Kyle Dzintars, Kayla Wood, Rikki Zeigen, and Joe Hutchins who come up with amazing ideas and then make them happen. This manual came out of our meetings and recognizing the needs of helping professionals who want to do play therapy at the highest level. My assistant Allison Meyers is a gift from the divine. Thank you, Allison, for anticipating what I need and when I need it. Ashley Lawton Converse is an assistant director at my clinical practice but that description does not do her justice. Thank you, Ashley, for your thoughtfulness, passion, dedication, your ripple effect is felt and appreciated.

Finally, I would like to thank my friends and family. I have some of the coolest, spunkiest, kindest girlfriends on the planet. Thank you for listening to my stories and caring about me enough to care about my profession. I am blessed with a family that supports where my purpose takes me. Thank you to my now adult-ish children, Leah and Andrew. You two make me so proud each and every day, certainly of what you do, but more importantly of who you are. Everyone should be lucky enough to have a partner whose love and support is unwavering. Thank you, Michael, for being my person. I love you.

ALSO BY JODI MULLEN

Raising Freakishly Well Behaved Kids: 20 principles for being the parent your child needs.

Child-Centered Play Therapy Workbook: A Self-Directed Guide for Professionals.

Naughty No More: A workbook to help children make good decisions.

How Play Therapists can Engage Parents & Professionals

Counseling Children: A Core Issues Approach.

Supervision can be playful: Techniques for Child and Play Therapist Supervisors.

Counseling children and adolescents through grief and loss.

ABOUT THE AUTHOR

Dr. Jodi Ann Mullen, PhD LMHC NCC RPT-S CCPT-Master is a professor at SUNY Oswego in the Counseling and Psychological Services Department where she is the coordinator of the Mental Health Counseling Program and Graduate Certificate Program in Play Therapy. She is a practicing licensed mental health counselor and play therapist with over 25 years experience as a helping professional. Dr. Mullen is the director and founder of Integrative Counseling Services, with offices in central New York. She is an international speaker, author, credentialed play therapist and play therapy supervisor. Dr. Mullen was the 2008 recipient of the Key Award for Professional Training and Education through the Association for Play Therapy. She is the proud Momma of Leah and Andrew.

Integrative Counseling Services, PLLC

www.integrativecounseling.us

ISBN   978-0-9796287-3-3

DISCOUNT CODE

Want to supplement your consultations with parents?

Check out Raising Freakishly Well Behaved Kids: 20 Principles for Becoming the Parent your Child Needs!

Use the following code to get 10% off your purchase from our website!

RFWBKPTBT

www.integrativecounseling.us/store

www.ingramcontent.com/pod-product-compliance
Lightning Source LLC
Chambersburg PA
CBHW080251030426
42334CB00023BA/2775